# THE UFO BOOK

# THE UFO BOOK

## BOOK

A CHRONOLOGICAL JOURNEY FROM CROP CIRCLES TO ROSWELL

## JOHN MICHAEL GREER

U

UNION
SQUARE
& CO.

NEW YORK

**UNION**
**SQUARE**
**& CO.**

**NEW YORK**

UNION SQUARE & CO. and the distinctive Union Square & Co. logo
are trademarks of Sterling Publishing Co., Inc.

Union Square & Co., LLC, is a subsidiary of
Sterling Publishing Co., Inc.

ISBN 978-1-4549-5685-3
ISBN 978-1-4549-5686-0 (e-book)

Library of Congress Control Number: 2024949122

For information about custom editions, special sales,
and premium purchases, please contact
specialsales@unionsquareandco.com.

Printed in China

2 4 6 8 10 9 7 5 3 1

unionsquareandco.com

Cover and interior design by Erik Jacobsen
Cover text set in Alba by Fontalicious, © Font Bros. www.fontbros.com
Cover illustrations by Aaron Lowell Denton
Image credits appear on page 208

# CONTENTS

# INTRODUCTION

## "Something is seen, but one doesn't know what."

That was how Swiss psychologist Carl Jung summed up the UFO controversy in 1958. It's still a valid description. Plenty of people have their own theories about what the mysterious objects seen in the sky might be, or must be, or certainly cannot be, but the proof that would confirm any of these theories is lacking.

Are unidentified flying objects (or, as the US government now likes to call them, UAPs, "unidentified anomalous phenomena") spaceships from other planets crewed by alien astronauts? Are they, as Jung himself believed, manifestations of the deep layers of our minds, bursting into sight to warn us of impending changes in consciousness? Are they the latest manifestation of those strange beings that people in ancient times called gods, spirits, and elves? Are they living creatures from the upper atmosphere, as some UFO researchers in the 1950s believed? Is the whole phenomenon, or some part of it, the product of deliberate fakery on the part of one or more governments, perhaps to conceal experimental aircraft, perhaps for some other reason? Or is it all just a matter of misperceptions, hallucinations, and hoaxes, as the skeptics claim?

In my previous book on the subject, *The UFO Chronicles*, I have tried to summarize the evidence and suggest some of the things that may be behind it. This book has a different purpose, however. In the pages that follow, I have set out to tell the story of the UFO phenomenon from ancient times to the present through 100 incidents. I have included sightings, close encounters, and abductions, as well as other events that have shaped the collective narrative concerning UFOs. The one thing I haven't done is attempt to explain what was behind any of the sightings. That, dear reader, is up to you.

Each of the events discussed in the pages that follow could easily be the subject of an entire book, and some of them have had books—sometimes many books—written about them. Others have been neglected by UFO researchers and skeptics alike. I could easily have filled ten books this size with UFO-related incidents, but I have tried to focus on those events that are well documented and have played a significant role in shaping public opinion about the phenomenon. The incidents included here cluster in space and time because UFOs are unevenly distributed;

**BELOW AND LEFT:**
Hazy photos of what
might be UAPs . . .

there are places and times where many
people see them, and others where they
are few and far between. Why? There are
theories, but once again, nobody knows.

As you read through these pages, I
encourage you to keep an open mind, to
be ready to look for further details on the
internet or in books, and to enjoy your own
vicarious close encounters with one of the
most astonishing mysteries of our time.

**—JOHN MICHAEL GREER**

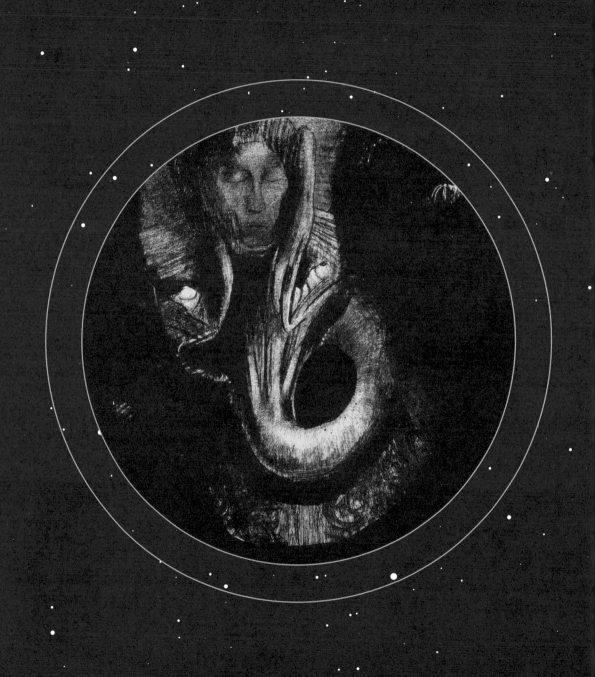

# MYSTERIOUS VISITORS

He emerged from the waters of the Persian Gulf at sunrise in full view of the astonished tribespeople: a mysterious living being with a scaled body like a fish but a face, hands, and feet like a human being. He spoke to the witnesses in their own language. He gave his name as Oannes. Day after day he returned to the shore and taught the tribespeople the arts of civilization but returned to the sea every night.

This is how the ancient writer Berossus described a close encounter with an alien intelligence. There are thousands of such stories preserved in the myths and legends of peoples around the world and throughout history. Some of these accounts include details that seem weirdly prescient in the light of more recent events. Many Native American cultures, for example, preserve tales of people who live in the sky and who occasionally descend to Earth and take people away with them—an eerie parallel to the alien abduction phenomenon that has played so important and baffling a role in UFO research circles.

Most modern scholars refer to these beings as gods, spirits, and culture heroes, and dismiss these accounts as empty fictions circulated by superstitious people. Even so skeptical a scientist as Carl Sagan, however, argued in one of his early books that the legend of Oannes might record a dim memory of human contact with nonhuman intelligences. Many other writers less committed to the intellectual status quo have raised similar questions about a wide range of other traditional stories. These questions are among the many unsolved riddles associated with the strange objects many people have seen in the sky over the centuries.

**SEE ALSO:** Voyagers from Magonia (815), The *Utsuro-Bune* Incident (1803), *Chariots of the Gods?* (1968)

WHEN DID EXTRATERRESTRIAL LIFE EMERGE?: This figure from Odilon Redon's "The Temptation of Saint Anthony" series sums up a quote from Oannes: "I, the first consciousness in Chaos, rose from the abyss to harden matter, to determine forms."

# SHIELDS AND LIGHTS IN THE HEAVENS

The ancient Romans were no strangers to unknown aerial phenomena, and some of their reports have a remarkably modern flavor. In his entry for 216 BCE, for example, the great Roman historian Livy reported that "shields" had been seen in the sky above the Italian town of Arpi. The Latin word that Livy used, *clipei*, was used for round bronze shields and could also simply mean metal disks of any kind. According to Julius Obsequens, a Roman scholar who studied anomalies, more shields were spotted fighting with each other in the sky above Amelia and Todi, near modern Rimini, in 103 BCE, and another flying shield was sighted over Tarquinia, near modern Viterbo, in 99 BCE, crossing the sky from west to east.

Strange lights were also spotted in the heavens by sharp-eyed Roman observers and chronicled by Roman writers. In 218 BCE, a light like the sun was observed in the night sky in several places in Italy, including Capua and Pisa. In 76 BCE, a Roman official and his entourage saw something that looked like a spark descending from the night sky; as it descended, it seemed to grow until it was as large as the moon. After a short time, it rose back up again into the sky, where it resembled a torch. In 187 CE, bright lights like stars were observed over Rome in the daytime, and in 195 CE, three starlike lights were seen from Rome close to the sun.

All these strange objects were interpreted by Roman intellectuals as omens from the gods. In terms of the ideas of their own time and culture, this was the logical explanation for them. One question that every modern investigator of unidentified aerial phenomena needs to keep in mind is how much of our interpretation of unknown lights and shapes in the sky may be equally a product of our time and culture.

**SEE ALSO:** Battle in the Skies (1561), The Foo Fighters (1944)

EARLY SIGHTINGS: This sixteenth-century book on comets records an unsettling display in the heavens.

# VOYAGERS FROM MAGONIA

According to contemporary records, medieval France was visited repeatedly by "cloudships" crewed by humanlike beings who came to gather up crops from the earth and carry them back to a distant region called Magonia. We know about these visitations primarily from the writings of one of the first known UFO skeptics, Archbishop Agobard of Lyons (769–840), who wrote a book titled *On Hail and Thunder* (in Latin, *De Grandine et Tonitruis*) condemning popular beliefs concerning Magonia and its cloudships. Agobard explained in his book:

> We have even seen several of these lunatics who, believing in the reality of such absurd things, exhibited before an assembled crowd four people in chains, three men and one woman, said to have descended from one of these ships. They had been holding them bound for several days when they brought them before me, followed by the crowd, in order to stone them.

Agobard was able to save the lives of the four people by pointing out that anyone who believed in Magonia must also believe in the power of sorcery. At that time, this belief was forbidden by the Church, and anyone affirming it was therefore liable to serious punishment! (It was not until four centuries later that theologians changed their minds on this point and set in motion the witchcraft persecutions of the late Middle Ages.)

The belief in cloudships from some distant place was not limited to the region around Lyons. Until the time of Charlemagne, who forbade the practice, French peasants used to try to ward off the depredations of the cloudships by setting up tall poles in their fields with magic parchments tied to the top. All across Europe in the early Middle Ages, stories of ships sailing in the sky were equally common.

**SEE ALSO:** Mysterious Visitors (5000 BCE), The *Utsuro-Bune* Incident (1803), Pancakes from Space? (1961), The Cussac Close Encounter (1967), *Chariots of the Gods?* (1968), The Rise of High Strangeness (1969)

CLOUDSHIPS OR FANTASY?: This Medieval illustration records a depiction that prompted both awe and skepticism.

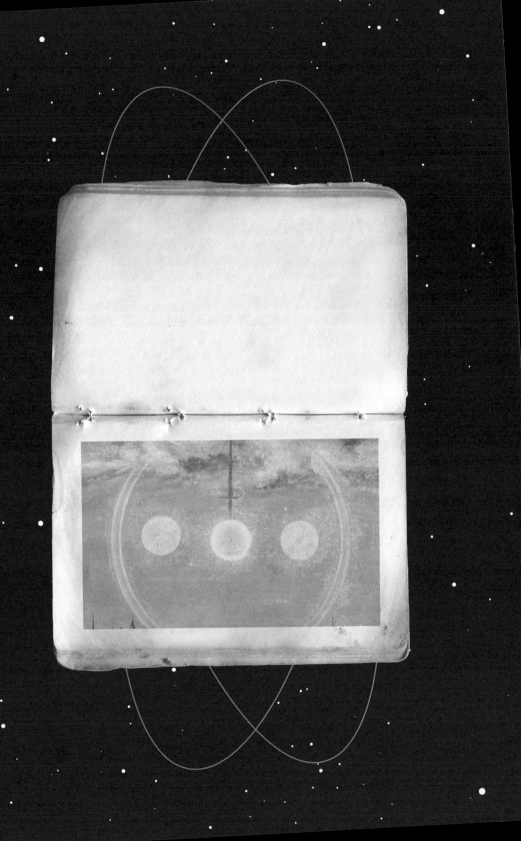

# THE BAODING
# SIGHTING

Mysterious flying objects also occur frequently in the records of imperial China. One classic sighting of a kind familiar to modern researchers was chronicled by Liu Yin, an influential scholar whose commentaries on the Confucian classics are still treasured. Just after dawn on June 3, 1277, while he was living just outside the village of Baoding in Hebei Province, he witnessed an unnerving spectacle in the heavens.

He woke before sunrise and looked out the window of his room to see a brilliant light crossing the Milky Way. Then, in the southern sky, three glowing objects appeared. Two moved away at high speed, but the third remained. Liu Yin made out five lights of varying brightness underneath it, while the upper surface was dome-shaped. As he watched, it moved in a zigzag fashion, like a falling leaf. Meanwhile, something surrounded by flames fell from another part of the sky. As the sun rose, the first object flew northward out of sight, but another object, shaped like a flat oval, descended suddenly out of a greenish cloud. It was surrounded by flames and rose and fell in the air.

Amazed by this spectacle, Liu Yin ran to the village to alert his friends, but as his friends came outside to look, the flying object disappeared. Afterward, baffled by the nature of the sighting, he wrote down a detailed account of the events of the morning in the hope that some other scholar would be able to explain the strange flying things he had seen. Three-quarters of a millennium later, we are not much closer to finding a convincing explanation, but some of the details of Liu Yin's sighting—especially the "falling leaf" motion, which has been reported many times by modern witnesses—make his account startlingly modern.

**SEE ALSO:** The Dinghai Sighting (1562), The Swamp Gas Incident (1966)

A BRILLIANT LIGHT CROSSING THE MILKY WAY: Accounts of unidentified anomalous phenomena were not uncommon in imperial China.

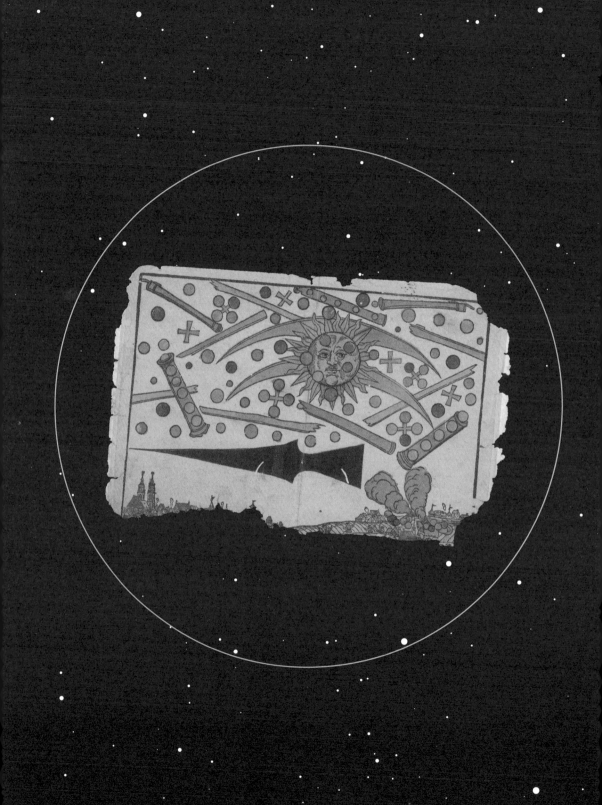

# BATTLE IN THE SKIES

The people of the free city of Nurem-berg, one of hundreds of quasi-independent statelets in the sprawl-ing Holy Roman Empire, were no strangers to warfare. Still, the battle that erupted in the skies above the city early in the morning of April 14, 1561, was as new to them as it was terrifying. According to a news broadsheet published later the same month, the strug-gle took place between 4:00 and 5:00 a.m. and was witnessed by many people in and around the city.

The incident began when witnesses on the ground observed two semicircular arcs like blood-red lunar crescents in the rising sun. Shortly thereafter, flying spheres—some red, some black, and some a mixture of the two colors—emerged from the sun and began to fight with one another. Cylindrical and cross-shaped objects then joined the struggle, darting in and out of the sun. As the struggle reached its peak, spheres, cylinders, and crosses alike plunged down onto the earth emitting great clouds of smoke as though they were burning. Next, a triangular black object like a huge spearhead appeared from the east and flew westward. This marked the end of the battle as far as the people of Nuremberg could tell.

Nuremberg was far from the only city in sixteenth-century Europe to witness such a spectacle. Five years later, on July 27 and 28 and then again on August 7, 1566, a similar event took place in the skies above the Swiss city of Basel and was duly recorded by the town newspaper. According to that account, once again red and black spheres participated in the struggle. Scholars of the period have noted that there are many other such events chronicled in the broadsheets and newspapers of central Europe during this period. No convincing explanation of these events has yet been offered.

**SEE ALSO:** Shields and Lights in the Heavens (216 BCE), The Foo Fighters (1944)

THE BATTLE ABOVE NUREMBERG: This sixteenth-century illustration was printed in a news notice and distributed to residents.

# THE DINGHAI SIGHTING

The middle years of the sixteenth century seem to have been a busy time for unidentified aerial phenomena. Just over a year after the remarkable events above Nuremberg, for example, villagers in Dinghai County in Zhejiang Province, China, observed a strange object descending out of the northwestern sky. The date was July 24, 1562; the time, a little after sunset. Witnesses said that the object resembled a *dou*, a traditional rice-measuring container; it had a pointed top, a rounded bottom colored yellow and white, and a maroon bracket on one side.

The object descended rapidly, surrounded by flames. Its light was so brilliant that witnesses could see the fine hairs on their skin. Just before it hit the ground, it suddenly rose higher in the air and then went up and down several times, sending shadows dancing. What happened to it then has not been explained in the one account of this sighting in a Western language. The descent of the strange object, however, was witnessed over an area more than five hundred miles across, and the accounts of witnesses were gathered by the imperial Chinese government and forwarded to the office that handled reports of omens and strange events.

As this suggests, ancient China was rich in reports of mysterious aerial phenomena. One collection of these reports lists no fewer than 741 UFO sightings between 139 BCE and 1918 CE. Very little of this material has yet been examined by UFO researchers in Western countries, and even less has been translated into Western languages. When the abundant Chinese UFO lore is finally compared with its Western equivalents, we may know much more about the history of the phenomena.

**SEE ALSO:** The Baoding Sighting (1277), The Tunguska Event (1908), The Kecksburg Crash (1965)

UAPS IN SIXTEENTH-CENTURY CHINA: Sightings were frequent during the period between 139 BCE and 1918 CE.

Drawn from the Original Picture by J.R. Penniman.

J. Cheney sculp.

# JOHN WINTHROP.

## FIRST GOVERNOR OF MASSACHUSETTS.

# THE MUDDY RIVER SIGHTING

Strange aerial objects also appeared in the area that would become the United States of America, starting long before the colonies revolted against Britain. John Winthrop, governor of the Puritan colony on Massachusetts Bay, recorded several classic sightings in his diary. The earliest was dated March 1, 1639. Earlier that year, Winthrop wrote, colonist James Everell and two others were in a rowboat on the aptly named Muddy River, a tributary of the Charles River.

That night, all three men saw a strange light in the sky. When first seen, it was about three yards across, or so the men estimated, but it contracted to the size and shape of a large pig and began to move "as swift as an arrow," back and forth between the Muddy River and the village of Charlestown two miles away. It kept up this movement for several hours and then vanished. When it disappeared, the three men found that somehow they had moved a mile upstream, with no memory of having rowed that distance against the current. This is one of the earliest known examples of the "missing time" syndrome now associated with abduction experiences.

Another set of strange nocturnal lights appears in an entry in Winthrop's diary dated January 18, 1644. Once again, three men were involved in this sighting, and they were traveling in a boat. About midnight, Winthrop noted, the three men saw two lights rising out of the water of Boston Harbor. The lights were the size and approximate shape of human beings. They flew over the town to South Point and then abruptly vanished.

Winthrop, a devout Puritan, interpreted these and other strange events in terms of the religion and folklore of his own era. Three centuries and many cultural changes would happen before anyone thought to identify them as evidence for visitors from outer space.

SEE ALSO: The Baoding Sighting (1277), The Barney and Betty Hill Abduction (1961), *Communion* (1987)

STRANGE NOCTURNAL LIGHTS: The first governor of Massachusetts, John Winthrop, recorded several sightings in his diary.

# THE ROBOZERO SIGHTING

nother intriguing early modern sighting of an unidentified aerial object took place in 1663 near the Russian village of Robozero. On Saturday, August 15, peasants from the region had gathered at the church in Robozero. Around noon, while the service was taking place, a loud noise was heard outside, and many people ran out to see what was happening. They sighted a glowing shape like a ball of fire, about 140 feet across, flying across the sky from the north. From its leading edge, two burning rays extended another 140 feet or so. It passed over the church and flew off toward a nearby lake.

Less than an hour later, the object was back, flying from the lake to the western sky, where it vanished briefly. Then it returned and hovered over Robozero for an hour and a half before disappearing again. Then word came that two fishermen who had been in a boat on the lake had suffered burns from the heat radiated by the object. They told others that they had seen the lake water illuminated to a depth of thirty feet, while the fish fled toward the shore to get away from the light and heat. They also said that the water appeared to be covered with rust under the reddish light from the object.

A local official, Ivachko Revskoi, learned about the sighting from a farmer, Levko Fedorov, and went to Robozero to investigate. The priests in the district confirmed that Fedorov's story was accurate, and Revskoi forwarded a detailed report to the monastery of St. Cyril, where it was entered into the records. This thoroughly modern UFO case remains among history's many unexplained sightings.

**SEE ALSO:** The Stadio Artemio Franchi Sighting (1954), The Westall School Sighting (1966), The Ariel School Close Encounter (1994)

BURNED BY FIRE FROM ABOVE: Fishermen near the Russian village of Robozero were injured after a sighting of a mysterious object in the sky.

# The Mowing-Devil:

## Or, Strange *NEWS* out of

# Hartford-shire.

Being a True Relation of a Farmer, who Bargaining
with a Poor *Mower*, about the Cutting down Three Half
Acres of Oats; upon the *Mower's* asking too much, the Farmer swore, *That the Devil should Mow it*, rather than He:
And so it fell out, that that very Night, the Crop of Oats
shew'd as if it had been all of a Flame; but next Morning
appear'd so neatly Mow'd by the Devil, or some Infernal Spirit, that no Mortal Man was able to do the like.
Also, How the said *Oats* ly now in the Field, and the Owner
has not Power to fetch them away.

Licensed, *August* 22th. 1678.

# THE MOWING DEVIL

rop circles are another aspect of the modern UFO phenomenon that can be traced back many centuries. One unusually well-documented example took place in Hertfordshire, England, in 1678. Like most early accounts of UFO-related phenomena, it was interpreted by the witnesses in terms of the folklore and religious beliefs of its own place and time, which focused on the Christian devil rather than aliens from distant planets.

The story, which was recorded in a cheap pamphlet at the time, ran as follows: A farmer in Hertfordshire wanted to hire a laborer to harvest three and a half acres of oats. The laborer he approached asked so high a wage, however, that the farmer swore that he would sooner let the devil mow the grain than have it done at that price. That night, witnesses saw what seemed to be flame rising from the oat field. The next morning, the oats had been mowed with supernatural neatness, and the farmer found that he was unable to take them from the field.

The picture in the pamphlet, a crude woodcut, shows a black humanoid figure with a scythe laying down the grain in a spiral pattern like the one commonly found in late-twentieth-century crop circles. The image, along with the story, led to the "mowing devil" incident being identified as one of the first recorded crop circles. The situation was not identical, however, since the oats in 1678 were cut rather than being bent, as in later crop circles. Nonetheless, the story of the mowing devil of Hertfordshire serves as another useful reminder that many aspects of the modern UFO experience go back far into antiquity.

SEE ALSO: The Tully Crop Circles (1966), The Circle Makers Unveiled (1991)

STRANGE NEWS OUT OF HERTFORDSHIRE: This English woodcut pamphlet was distributed to the residents of the town after an unexplained occurrence.

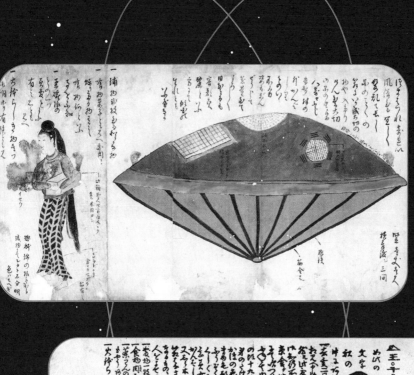

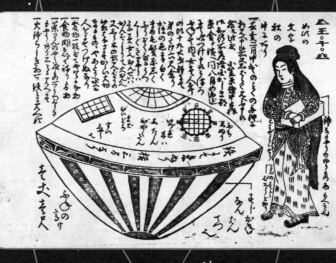

# THE *UTSURO-BUNE* INCIDENT

One of the odder events in the Japanese chronicles is the story of the *Utsuro-bune*, or "hollow boat," a saucer-shaped craft that appeared on the shores of Hitachi Province in Japan on February 22, 1803. The upper surface was the red color of lacquered rosewood, with several transparent windows in it, and the underside was plated with metal. Inside was a young woman, eighteen to twenty years old, dressed in long, smooth garments of unknown material. She had red hair with long white extensions of artificial hair braided into it, and her skin was a very pale pink color.

Local fishermen succeeded in hauling the craft to shore, opened it, and tried to communicate with the woman. However, she did not understand Japanese, nor did any of the fishermen understand the language she spoke. She appeared friendly and polite but clutched a cubical box of some pale substance in both hands and would not let anyone else touch it. Inside the craft were two unusually soft carpets of an unknown type and a store of food.

At the time, Japan was isolated from the rest of the world by order of its rulers, the Tokugawa shoguns, who hoped to keep their nation free of European colonial empires. Strict laws prohibited Japanese people from fraternizing with foreigners. According to one account, the fishermen thus put the woman back into the *Utsuro-bune*, hauled it back out into the open ocean, and sent it on its way. Another version claims that the *Utsuro-bune* was sent back out to sea, but the woman stayed behind in the fishing village and lived to an old age there.

Does this odd story have anything to do with UFOs? Several Japanese researchers have pointed to the similarity between the *Utsuro-bune* and the saucer-shaped craft seen in the skies elsewhere in the world in recent years, and suggested a connection.

**SEE ALSO:** Mysterious Visitors (5000 BCE), Voyagers from Magonia (815), *Chariots of the Gods?* (1968)

THE HOLLOW SHIP: Four separate texts make reference to what might have been a close encounter, including these two accounts, the lower written in 1844 by Nagahashi Matajirou.

The Mysterious Flying Light That Hovered Over St. Mary's College, Oakland, and Then Started for San Francisco. It Is Exactly Like That Described by Sacramentans, and Similar to the Cut Published a Few Days Ago in "The Call" From a Description Furnished by One Who Saw It.

# THE COMING OF
# THE AIRSHIPS

**1896**

J. B. Ligon, a resident of Beaufort, Texas, didn't expect to stumble across an enduring mystery on April 19, 1897, when he and his son Charles spotted moving lights in a nearby pasture and went to investigate. Instead of cattle rustlers, they encountered four men standing by a grounded airship. The men claimed to have flown there from Iowa and asked for two buckets of water. The Ligons gave them the water, and the men took off and flew away.

The Ligons weren't the only Americans who saw airships in 1896 and 1897. Thousands of witnesses in twenty American states spotted them—cigar-shaped objects high in the air, many of them with bright lights. Most witnesses assumed these shapes were experimental airships. More than a dozen people, like the Ligons, had their own close encounters with airship pilots during those two years. In most of these encounters, the pilots insisted that they were inventors who had created a working airship and would soon reveal their invention to the world.

No such revelation ever happened. Instead, over the decades that followed, inventors in half a dozen countries painstakingly designed and tested the technologies that would make flying machines work and slowly reached the point where they could equal the performance of the phantom airships of 1896 and 1897. To this day, no one knows what was behind the airships that the Ligons and so many other people saw. Some researchers have dismissed the reports as hoaxes; some have argued that a secret airship program in advance of publicly known technology may actually have existed during those years— but even when the airships were first sighted, there were a few people who speculated that they may have come from other worlds.

SEE ALSO: The Return of the Airships (1909), Airships Again (1913)

PHANTOM AIRSHIPS: This article from the November 22, 1896, edition of the newspaper *The San Francisco Call* recounts a sighting over Sacramento, California.

# THE AURORA CRASH

Newspapers around the United States were still full of stories about mystery airships on the morning of April 17, 1897, when an airship crashed into the windmill on Judge J. S. Proctor's property near the little town of Aurora, Texas. Around 6:00 a.m. it was sighted by numerous witnesses, flying north at a speed of only ten or twelve miles an hour and sinking slowly toward the ground. When it collided with the windmill, it exploded, scattering debris over several acres of farmland and wrecking the windmill.

According to contemporary newspaper accounts, townsfolk ran to the site. The account in the *Dallas Morning News* two days later included unsettling details: the wreckage of the craft appeared to be made of an unknown metal, "resembling somewhat a mixture of aluminum and silver," and the airship's sole occupant was lying dead on the ground, with papers on his body written in unknown hieroglyphics. "While his remains are badly disfigured," the paper claimed enough of the original has been picked up to show that he was "not an inhabitant of this world." A local astronomy buff suggested that the pilot was an inhabitant of Mars.

In the midst of the airship furor, the Aurora crash got little attention. Most of a century later, UFO investigators looking into the airship phenomenon found the story and went to investigate. No trace of the mysterious metal or the hieroglyphic writings turned up, and the grave of the alien pilot proved equally elusive. Many writers on the subject have dismissed the entire story as a hoax, but conclusive evidence has yet to emerge. The most remarkable thing about the Aurora crash in retrospect, however, is how closely the account prefigured news reports of the Roswell crash just over fifty years later.

**SEE ALSO:** The Tunguska Event (1908), The Roswell Crash (1947), The Kecksburg Crash (1965), The Shag Harbour Crash (1967), The Megaplatanos Crash (1990), The Varginha Close Encounters (1996)

SITE OF THE "ALIEN GRAVE": This stone, engraved with carvings of the spaceship seen over Aurora, marks the final resting place of an extraterrestrial commonly referred to as "Ned" by residents of the town.

# THE TUNGUSKA EVENT

The Tunguska River valley is located in an isolated region of central Siberia, north of Lake Baikal. At 7:17 a.m. on the morning of June 30, 1908, an elongated luminous object came from the southeast and detonated over the valley north of the town of Vanovara. The fireball incinerated eight hundred thousand acres of timber, and five hundred reindeer near ground zero were roasted alive where they stood. Windows shattered 120 miles away. Barometers in London tracked the shock wave as it circled the globe twice, and over the next few nights the skies in western Europe glowed so brightly that people could read the newspaper without any other light.

Current estimates of the explosion give it a force between twelve and thirty megatons—the biggest blast on Earth until the invention of the hydrogen bomb. Scientists at the time assumed that a meteor must have been responsible. Yet when the first geologists reached the area, they discovered no crater and no meteor fragments. Whatever detonated over the Tunguska valley must have blown up in the air. A comet? Maybe, but a comet large enough to cause such a disaster would have been visible to astronomers long before it plunged into Earth's atmosphere, and there were many amateur and professional astronomers looking for comets in 1908.

UFO researchers have offered an alternative suggestion. They point out that Russian researchers in 1959 and 1960 found unexplained mutations in plants and animals in the area and an unusual amount of radioactive cesium in local tree rings from 1908. Is it possible that a nuclear-powered spacecraft from some other world might have blown up over Siberia that morning? They suggest that this is worth considering—and no one has yet found another explanation that accounts for all the data.

**SEE ALSO:** The Roswell Crash (1947), The Kecksburg Crash (1965), The Shag Harbour Crash (1967), The Megaplatanos Crash (1990), The Varginha Close Encounters (1996)

THE SITE OF THE EXPLOSION: This map depicts the area in Siberia in which a massive explosion incinerated hundreds of thousands of acres of land.

# THE RETURN OF THE AIRSHIPS

The explosion over Tunguska may have been an omen of sorts, for the next year the mystery airships returned. Airships were in the news just then; Count Ferdinand von Zeppelin's epochal flight over Lake Constance on July 2, 1909, was splashed all over the news media, and many other countries had launched their own airship programs. The whereabouts of the few known airships at that time, however, were closely tracked by reporters and spies. None of them appear to be involved in the second great wave of unknown airship sightings, which spread over Europe and Australia starting in early 1909.

England was the first place visited by the mysterious airships. A constable in Peterborough spotted one on the morning of March 23, and for the next two months sightings poured in from across the British Isles; East Anglia, Essex, Wales, and Northern Ireland all had reports. In some cases all the witnesses saw was a light in the sky, while others heard the sound of an engine. Still others watched a cigar shape moving through the air, while a few had what would later be called a close encounter of the third kind with a landed craft and crew members.

Even more dramatic sightings, however, were reported from New Zealand and Australia. A schoolteacher and her students in Kelso, on New Zealand's South Island, witnessed a black cigar-shaped craft maneuvering high in the air on July 23. Other witnesses on South Island sighted the same craft, or a very similar one, at various times over the weeks that followed. In early August, the mystery craft moved operations to Australia. All through the month of August, witnesses reported cigar-shaped craft or moving lights in the sky in New South Wales, Tasmania, and Western Australia. Thereafter the craft vanished—for a time.

**SEE ALSO:** The Coming of the Airships (1896), Airships Again (1913)

AN AIRSHIP OVER PETERBOROUGH:  An airship, as seen over Peterborough Cathedral by Constable Kettle, in March 1909.

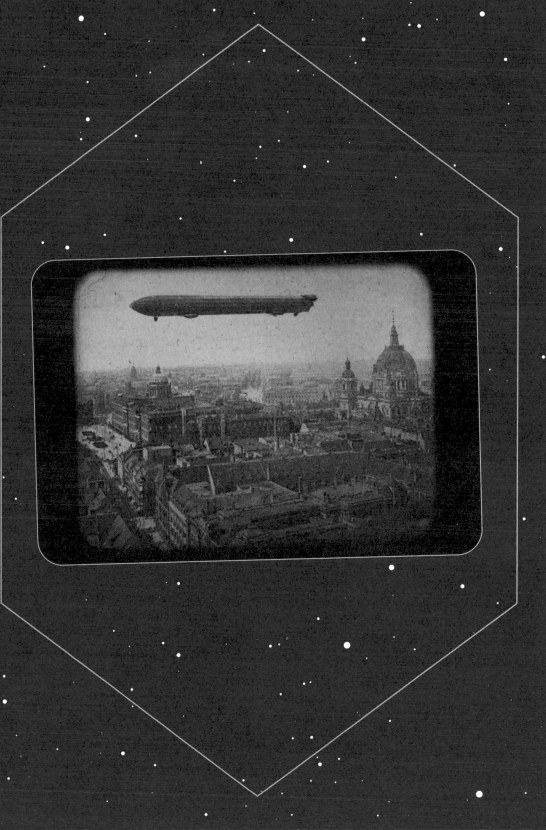

# AIRSHIPS AGAIN

On the first months of 1913, the phantom airships showed that they weren't finished with their mysterious maneuvers. On January 17 of that year, more than a dozen people spotted an airship flying over southern Wales and the nearby English border counties. Hundreds of people in the same region watched an unusually bright light maneuvering high in the air on February 5. On February 21, the mystery craft began a series of visits to the skies above Yorkshire, where thousands of people witnessed an aerial light and some claimed to see a long, cigar-shaped body at high altitude. Sightings continued almost daily in the area for the next week and then declined. A few more sightings took place in April, June, August, and September.

All this took place at a time of rising international tension, as the German empire positioned itself to confront Britain and its allies. The German military was investing heavily in airships, and while Britain had its own airship program, the Germans were thought to be well ahead in the airship race. Most witnesses assumed that they were seeing German zeppelins scouting out Britain's defenses or even landing spies and saboteurs. The British press was full of frantic editorials demanding that someone do something to stop the sinister German craft.

Once the First World War was over and Germany's military records were available to Allied researchers, however, it turned out that none of the sightings could be attributed to German airships. Records from the other nations that had airship programs at the same time yielded the same results. Skeptics have blamed the entire phenomenon on mass hysteria and mistaken sightings of planets and bright stars; other researchers, less dismissive, have noted that cigar-shaped UFOs played an important role later in the history of the phenomenon.

**SEE ALSO:** The Coming of the Airships (1896), The Return of the Airships (1909)

IN THE AGE OF ZEPPELINS: During this period of time, many unexplained sightings assigned features to airships that resembled military zeppelins, like this one in the sky over Berlin in a photo from 1913.

# THE MYSTERY PLANES

In 1914, aeroplanes (as they were called then) were a new technology, fragile, balky, and experimental. The armies of most major powers were exploring their potential, but most military aircraft stayed in Europe, close to the war most people expected to break out. In South Africa, thousands of miles away, there was not a single functioning aircraft or even an airfield. That helped spark a general panic when airplanes—or lights that were interpreted as airplanes—started being sighted there in August of 1914, while Europe was plunging into war.

The first sightings were on the night of August 13–14, near Cape Town. Several witnesses spotted what they thought was a biplane circling over Table Bay on the evening of the 13th, and more witnesses spotted it before dawn on the 14th flying over the Cape Peninsula. That evening, thirteen people watched a bright light moving through the sky over Riversdale. On the night of the 16th, fifteen more people saw an aircraft carrying a bright light flying over Worcester. The nights of the 19th and 20th brought sightings from all over the Cape Town region; most witnesses reported a bright light in the sky, but some claimed to see an airplane carrying the light. The sightings peaked then and gradually stopped in early September.

Skeptics insisted that the witnesses had simply seen and misidentified the planet Venus, which was visible and very bright during those nights. Most South Africans assumed instead that the German military detachment in Namibia, then a German colony, had sent planes over to spy on South Africa's defenses. There were three German planes in Namibia at that time, but none of them had the range to get to Cape Town and back without landing to refuel, much less to spend hours night after night hovering over South Africa. No one yet knows for sure what the witnesses saw.

SEE ALSO: Scandinavia's Phantom Flyers (1933)

VENUS, OR . . . ?: This photo depicts the illuminated planet—was it, as skeptics believed, the reason so many thought they had seen an unidentified craft?

31

# THE BOOK OF THE DAMNED

Some intellectual revolutions are launched by colorful figures who lead exciting lives. Then there was Charles Fort, who looked like an amiable walrus and spent most of his time in public libraries or sitting behind his desk at home. He was a journalist in his younger years, but an inheritance gave him the chance to retire from that trade and devote the rest of his life to pursuing his real passion: chronicling data that had been excluded from official scientific research because it was simply too weird.

Then, as now, the scientific establishment had a bad habit of paying attention to evidence that supported its preconceived ideas and ignoring anything that contradicted the conventional wisdom. As a newspaperman, Fort had witnessed many examples of scientists insisting that their preferred explanations were correct, even at the expense of the facts. That experience drove his great project. His four books—

*The Book of the Damned* (1919), *New Lands* (1923), *Lo!* (1931), and *Wild Talents* (1932)—presented a parade of impossible facts to prove that scientists knew much less about the universe than they thought.

Unknown aerial objects and flying lights filled a significant number of Fort's pages. All through the nineteenth and early twentieth centuries, people witnessed strange things in the skies and reported their experiences to newspapers and scientific journals. Since no one knew what the lights were, all such accounts were grist for Fort's mill. His books are thus some of the best available resources for early UFO sightings—and he was also one of the first influential writers to suggest that the strange lights were piloted craft from another planet.

**SEE ALSO:** *When Prophecy Fails* (1954), *Chariots of the Gods?* (1968), *Communion* (1987), *Behold a Pale Horse* (1991)

FACT IS STRANGER THAN FICTION: The writings of Charles Fort (1874–1932) give us some excellent early records of brushes with the unknown.

# SCANDINAVIA'S PHANTOM FLYERS

The county of Västerbotten in northern Sweden is a rugged and heavily forested region just below the Arctic Circle, close to the border with Norway. In the late autumn of 1933, it had one airplane, an ambulance plane that was grounded for repairs. That left government officials in the region baffled when witnesses began to see flying lights moving along the valleys that connected the region with Norway. Police and customs agents investigated at once, guessing that smugglers were using the isolated region to bring contraband into Sweden, but they found no evidence of conventional aircraft in the area.

Sightings continued into the early months of 1934. Some witnesses saw planes, which they described as large, gray, and unmarked. Others simply spotted flying lights. The nights of January 8 and 9, 1934, the peak period of the "phantom flyers," had more than forty reports each. The Swedish air force, Flygvapnet, sent planes to the region but found nothing. Meanwhile, Swedish military officials contacted their equivalents in Norway and Finland and found that similar reports were being made in both countries. In all, some 487 sightings of unknown aircraft were reported from the three Scandinavian countries in the winter of 1933–34, of which one hundred were considered credible.

The phenomenon wound up before the end of that winter. In the winter of 1936–37, however, the phantom flyers were back for a second visit. Hundreds more sightings were reported, and the behavior of the unknown flying objects was just as evasive and puzzling as before. Were they secret planes from the Soviet Air Force or Nazi Germany's Luftwaffe, spying out the territory around northern Sweden's rich iron mines? Or was something genuinely strange going on? To this day, no one knows.

**SEE ALSO:** The Mystery Planes (1914), The Ghost Rockets (1946)

UFOS IN SNOWY SCANDINAVIA: A sunset in Västerbotten, Sweden, gives us a taste of the environment in which so many sightings were recorded.

# CORAL LORENZEN'S FIRST SIGHTING

On 1934, Barron, Wisconsin, was a small farm town of fifteen hundred people. At that time, airplanes were still so new that the arrival of a barnstormer in a field near town, offering airplane rides in a surplus military plane, was an event to be talked about for years thereafter. That was where nine-year-old Coral Lorenzen and two of her friends were playing one summer day when a strange object came into sight in the sky to the southwest.

Writing about the event later, Lorenzen described the object as shining white, shaped like an open umbrella without ribs or spurs, and about the apparent size of a dime held at arm's length. One of her friends thought that it might be a parachute, but the three girls could see no ropes, lines, or parachutist beneath it. They watched the object as it drifted slowly overhead with a curious undulating motion. Some twenty seconds after it first appeared, it vanished beyond the northern horizon. Lorenzen went home and told her father, who asked around; nobody else had seen the object, and no parachute was found north of Barron.

This would have been just one more ordinary sighting, the kind of event that earned a paragraph or two in one of Charles Fort's books, except that it awakened in Coral Lorenzen a lifelong interest in mysterious aerial objects. As an adult, she became a reporter for the *Green Bay Press-Gazette* in Wisconsin, placing many stories about unidentified aerial phenomena in its pages. In 1952, after she and dozens of other people sighted a silver ellipsoid hovering above Sturgeon Bay, she and her husband, Jim, founded the Aerial Phenomena Research Organization (APRO), which became one of the leading independent research centers for UFO studies and did much to publicize the phenomena.

**SEE ALSO:** NICAP Investigates the Phenomenon (1956)

FOUNDERS OF APRO: A childhood encounter led Coral Lorenzen, right, to found the Aerial Phenomena Research Organization with her husband, Jim (left).

# THE INVENTION OF FLYING SAUCERS

He could almost have passed for a little green man himself. Crippled in a childhood accident, tiny even as an adult, Raymond Palmer took refuge in science fiction. After making a name for himself as one of the founders of science fiction fandom, he was recruited by the Ziff-Davis chain of pulp magazines in 1938 to edit the failing monthly *Amazing Stories*. Palmer knew his audience better than anyone else in the business and filled the magazine's pages with trashy but entertaining stories of interplanetary adventure, making *Amazing Stories* the most popular and profitable of all the science fiction pulps.

In the process, he took the image of the flying disk out of earlier pulp magazines and made it an enduring icon. Back in 1915, one of pulp pioneer Hugo Gernsback's magazines had featured a disk-shaped aircraft. In the years that followed, flying disks appeared now and then on the covers of science fiction pulps, but it was Palmer who turned flying saucers into one of the standard images of future technology, splashing them in lurid colors across the covers of many issues.

This was far from the only detail of the UFO phenomenon to show up in science fiction in advance of the first great wave of sightings. Such staples of UFO lore as dwarfish aliens with big heads, extraterrestrials abducting humans for breeding purposes, and automobile electrical systems shutting down in the presence of flying saucers all showed up in pulp science fiction many years before people began experiencing them. No one knows why.

When maverick UFO researcher John Keel later described Palmer as "the man who invented flying saucers," he was only exaggerating a little. Without Palmer, the phenomenon might have taken a very different shape.

**SEE ALSO:** The Shaver Mystery (1945), The Phenomenon Predicted (1946), The Arnold Sighting (1947)

LITTLE GREEN MEN: This issue of *Amazing Stories* from March 1939 is packaged in a typical example of the fantastic science fiction art that became popular in mid century America; this one is by painter Robert Fuqua.

# THE FOO FIGHTERS

On the autumn of 1944, the skies of Europe were ablaze with war. British bomber fleets and American night fighter squadrons plunged into the airspace above occupied Europe to battle the Luftwaffe and bomb German cities. Allied aircrews by then were used to German fighter planes and antiaircraft cannon fire, but October brought something new and unexpected: spheres of glowing light or flame in red, orange, or white that followed their planes while aloft.

The first thought of the Allied air commands was that some new German secret weapon had been deployed, but the balls of light did not attempt any hostile action. They simply followed the planes, sometimes flying in close formation, sometimes veering wildly through the air. They appeared without warning and vanished without a trace. At first they were called "Kraut fireballs," but an American night fighter crewman who was a fan of the popular comic strip Smokey Stover borrowed a nonsense word used by one of the strip's characters and started calling them "foo fighters." American and British media picked up on the name, and it stuck.

Later researchers discovered that the first foo fighters were spotted by British aircrews over the Balkans beginning in April 1942, but the phenomenon did not become common until November 1944. Witnesses in the Pacific war also reported glowing objects in the sky, but these generally hovered in place for long periods rather than engaging in the aerobatic maneuvers that made the foo fighters famous. After the war, it turned out that Luftwaffe pilots had seen them, too, and were just as puzzled by them as their Allied counterparts. While claims have been made that they could have been a top-secret German experimental weapon, no evidence for this has yet been made public. The real cause of the foo fighters remains unknown.

**SEE ALSO:** Shields and Lights in the Heavens (216 BCE), Battle in the Skies (1561)

MYSTERIOUS BALL OF LIGHT: This photo shows what is believed to be a "foo fighter" in May 1945, near Karnten, Germany.

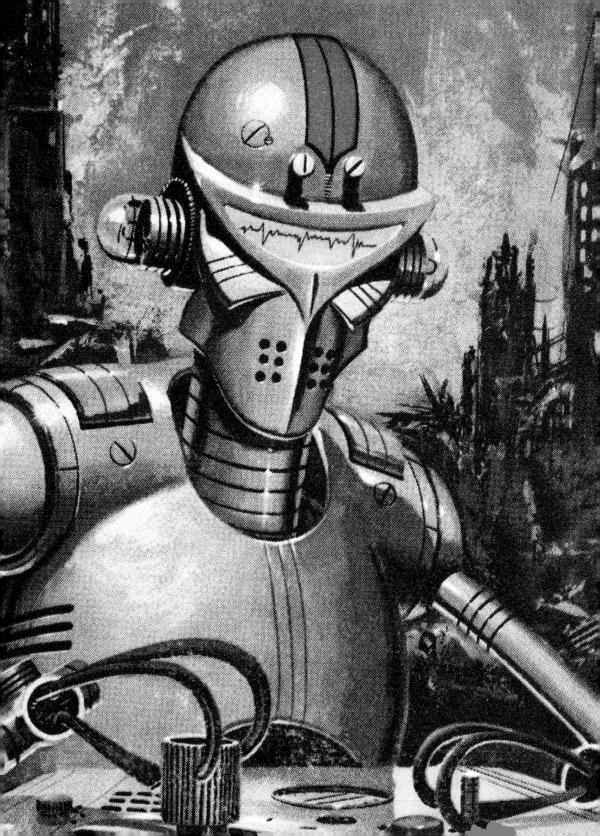

# THE SHAVER MYSTERY

Strange things were moving through the deep places of the modern mind as the Second World War came to an end. Some of them bubbled up in 1944 when Raymond Palmer, still editing *Amazing Stories*, read a strange narrative he'd received in the mail. The author was a welder named Richard Shaver who heard voices in his head when he operated welding gear. The voices told him of a hidden network of tunnels deep underground inhabited by evil dwarfs calls deros—short for "detrimental robots"—who used telepathic rays to torment unwary humans.

Palmer, recognizing this as pulp-fiction gold, rewrote the narrative and published it under the title "I Remember Lemuria!" in the March 1945 issue. The issue in which it appeared sold out. Palmer immediately contacted Shaver for more material and ran everything Shaver provided. *Amazing Stories* doubled its circulation.

Then readers began sending in letters about Shaver's stories. They didn't treat those as fiction, either. Many of them had their own encounters with deros to report, and the "Shaver Mystery" took on a life of its own. For the next two and a half years, most of the core themes of the UFO phenomena—strange flying objects, dwarfish creatures obsessed with human sexuality, abduction narratives, sinister underground bases, government cover-ups, and more—took center stage in discussions of the Shaver Mystery.

Palmer fed the flames with a steady drumbeat of stories by Shaver and others and with a letters column in each issue of the magazine packed with reader accounts of dero experiences. Finally, he got permission from his bosses in the Ziff-Davis pulp magazine chain to devote an entire issue to the subject. That issue was on newsstands around the country the day that Kenneth Arnold climbed into his airplane and launched UFOs into the limelight.

SEE ALSO: The Invention of Flying Saucers (1938), The Phenomenon Predicted (1946), The Arnold Sighting (1947)

SCIENCE FACT OR FICTION?: Were tales of robots living under the surface of the earth true, or simply a product of Robert Shaver's imagination?

# THE PHENOMENON PREDICTED

By the time the Second World War ended, the idea of life on other planets had become widely accepted throughout the world's industrial nations. Partly this resulted from science fiction's role in popular culture, and partly from the rapid progress of science itself. In a world still reeling from the nuclear explosions at Hiroshima and Nagasaki, the idea that human beings would soon cross outer space to other planets was hard to dismiss out of hand, and the idea that beings from other worlds might visit us became equally plausible.

Yet there were other, stranger reasons why the concept of communication with other worlds was on many minds at that time. In 1946 and early 1947, several influential American occultists suddenly began to announce that a visitation from space would begin soon. One of them was Meade Layne. An initiate of the Hermetic Order of the Golden Dawn, the most influential occult society of the time, Layne was an important figure in the California occult scene. He founded the Borderland Sciences Research Association (BSRA), a network of dissident researchers interested in magic and alternative science, which still exists today.

One of Layne's associates was a spirit medium named Mark Probert. In 1946, the Inner Circle, the group of spirits who spoke through Probert, informed Layne and others that strange craft would soon be seen in Earth's skies. Similar predictions surfaced elsewhere and found eager listeners. In response, people began to watch the skies, waiting for some sign of visitors from another world—and Probert's prediction was fulfilled the following year, when Kenneth Arnold's epochal sighting ushered in the modern era of UFOs.

**SEE ALSO:** The Invention of Flying Saucers (1938), The Shaver Mystery (1945), The Arnold Sighting (1947)

SPACE AGE SUSPICION: In an era of rapidly expanding technology, such as this V-2 rocket, it wouldn't have been hard to envision extraterrestrial craft making contact with Earth.

# THE GHOST ROCKETS

The Second World War had been over for less than a year, and the Soviet Union and the Western Allies were facing off over the smoldering wreckage of Germany, when observers in Sweden and Finland started seeing strange things flying over their countries: cigar- or missile-shaped craft moving at high speeds. The two long-range missiles Germany had fielded during the war, the V-1 cruise missile and the V-2 ballistic missile, saw much discussion in the newspapers at that time, so these unidentified flying craft were soon labeled "ghost rockets," *Spökraketer* in Swedish.

More than two thousand sightings of ghost rockets were reported by Swedish and Finnish witnesses between February 26, when they were first sighted, and the end of the year; the peak days for sightings were August 9 and 11. Two hundred of the ghost rockets were also detected on radar, and several were photographed, though the photos showed only contrails at high altitude. When one of the ghost rockets crashed, plunging into Lake Kölmjärv in Sweden on July 19, 1946, the Swedish military sent divers into the lake. They found the lake bottom disturbed, but the craft, whatever it might have been, left no traces behind.

At first, mass media and government officials speculated that Soviet scientists had taken over the V-2 base at Peenemünde, in the Soviet sector of Germany, and were testing rockets there. When this explanation failed to fit observed facts, the ghost rockets were redefined as meteorites. Not until the early twenty-first century did declassified papers reveal that some of the ghost rockets had been highly classified spy plane flights snooping on the Soviet Union—but it is far from certain that all the 1946 sightings can be assigned to that cause.

**SEE ALSO:** Scandinavia's Phantom Flyers (1933)

UFO OVER LAPLAND: When photographer Erik Reuterswürd captured this "ghost rocket," he believed it was a meteor, but when the image was released by the Swedish army, they left it up for interpretation.

47

# THE ARNOLD SIGHTING

When Kenneth Arnold climbed aboard his plane in Shelton, Washington, on the afternoon of June 24, 1947, he had no idea he was about to give unknown aerial objects a lasting place in the collective imagination of our age. He meant to fly from Shelton to Pendleton, Oregon, and take part in the search for a downed airplane near Mount Rainier en route. About three minutes after he reached cruising altitude, however, he spotted nine unknown objects in the air north of him, moving at a speed no earthly craft at that time could equal. They looked like nothing Arnold, an experienced observer, had ever seen before: crescent shapes of polished metal. They traveled close to the mountaintops, hugging the terrain and dipping from side to side as they flew.

When he touched down at Yakima, Washington, to refuel an hour and a half later, he mentioned his sighting to other pilots. Word spread so quickly that by the time he reached Pendleton, Oregon, later that afternoon, a small crowd was waiting for him. Trying to explain his sighting to journalists, he said that the mysterious craft flew "like a saucer if you skip it across water." Some unknown newspaper editor promptly revised that description into the catchy phrase "flying saucer."

Over the days that followed, as word of Arnold's sighting spread through the national media, people all over the United States started watching the skies. Many of them spotted, and some photographed, silver dots at high altitude moving from west to east. These widespread sightings gave the disks a lasting presence in popular culture that phantom airships, "foo fighters," and deros never had. Those earlier mysteries dropped out of popular culture as soon as they stopped appearing, but flying saucers seized an enduring place, first in the American imagination and then in that of the whole world.

SEE ALSO: The Phenomenon Predicted (1946), The Roswell Crash (1947)

ORIGINATOR OF THE TERM "FLYING SAUCER": Kenneth Arnold standing beside the aircraft on which he was flying when he saw something strange on June 24, 1947.

# THE ROSWELL CRASH

Rancher W. W. "Mac" Brazel wasn't sure what to make of the debris he found scattered across his land in June 1947. On July 5, he drove into the nearest town, Roswell, New Mexico, and for the first time heard about the flying disks that had been sighted by Kenneth Arnold and others. That sent him back to his property, where he gathered some of the debris and took it back to the sheriff's office in Roswell. The sheriff called Roswell Army Airfield, which sent two officers to investigate. They gathered the debris and went back to base, where publicity officer Walter Haut announced to the media that the military had recovered the remains of a flying disk.

The next day, the army backtracked, insisting that the debris was merely the remains of a weather balloon. The media dropped the story. Over the years that followed, UFO investigators kept probing, and rumors began to spread that the debris from the Roswell crash included the corpses of alien beings killed in the crash. By the mid-1960s, some UFO researchers were claiming that the US government had alien bodies from a crashed saucer in cold storage at Wright-Patterson Air Force Base in Ohio. Beginning in 1978, several dozen people who either had or claimed to have had contact with the Roswell crash went public, claiming that the wreckage was extraterrestrial in origin.

By 1994, Roswell was among the world's most famous UFO incidents, and a fog of competing stories and theories surrounded it. In that year, the US Air Force released documents claiming to show that what crashed at Roswell was balloon-borne gear from Project Mogul, a top-secret program that snooped on Russian nuclear tests. US government credibility had fallen so low by that point that few people accepted the new claim.

**SEE ALSO:** The Aurora Crash (1897), The Tunguska Event (1908), The Kecksburg Crash (1965), The Shag Harbour Crash (1967), The Rendlesham Forest Landing (1980), The Megaplatanos Crash (1990), The Varginha Close Encounters (1996)

WELCOME TO UFO COUNTRY: This sign, erected in 2017, welcomes visitors to Roswell, New Mexico.

# THE MANTELL INCIDENT

The phones started ringing at Fort Knox, Kentucky, just after noon on January 7, 1948. People in the nearby towns of Madisonville, Owensboro, and Irvington reported seeing a white circular object in the air, 250 to 300 feet in diameter. At 1:45 p.m., officers on duty at the Fort Knox airport control tower spotted the object. Witnesses at two other military bases in the region also saw the object in the distance, describing it as cone-shaped with a rounded top.

Four Mustang fighter planes of the Kentucky Air National Guard were already in the air, and the Fort Knox tower told them to investigate the object. As the planes approached, the object began to climb rapidly. Once it rose above 22,500 feet, the other planes turned back, but one plane piloted by Captain Thomas F. Mantell continued the chase.

Mantell was a veteran flyer who had won the Distinguished Flying Cross and the Air Medal while serving in the Second World War. He radioed the tower, saying that the object he was chasing appeared to be metallic and of enormous size. Shortly thereafter, the control tower lost contact with Mantell. His body was found in the wreckage of his airplane later that day.

Air Force investigators immediately started insisting that Mantell and the others had been chasing the planet Venus, and Mantell flew too high and blacked out from lack of oxygen. Venus is all but invisible in broad daylight, however, and would have been hidden by a thick layer of haze that day. Later, several investigators suggested that Mantell might have been chasing one of the navy's high-altitude balloon experiments, which were top secret in 1948. No one has yet been able to document a specific test in that area, but many of the balloon experiments in question remain classified to this day.

SEE ALSO: The Valentich Disappearance (1978)

CHASING THE UNEXPLAINED: This illustration depicts Captain Thomas Mantell pursuing an unidentified metallic object in 1948.

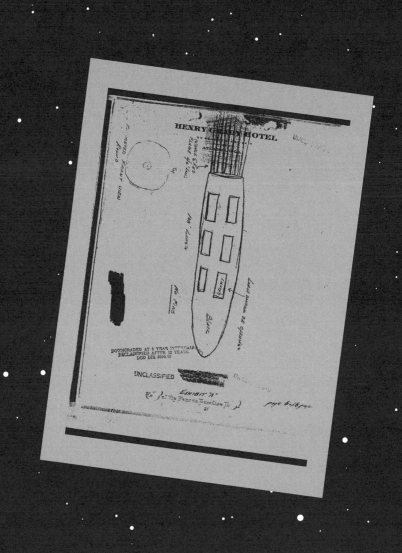

# THE CHILES-WHITTED SIGHTING

On the early hours of July 24, 1948, an Eastern Air Lines DC-3 with pilot Clarence Chiles and copilot John Whitted in the cabin was flying toward Atlanta, Georgia. The night was clear, with the moon shining through high scattered clouds. At approximately 2:45 a.m., Chiles noticed a dull red glow above and ahead of the plane and saw an unknown object coming out of the glow. He called Whitted's attention to the object, and they watched it for between ten and fifteen seconds as it shot past the DC-3 then flew upward at very high speed until it was lost to sight.

According to Chiles and Whitted, the object was cigar-shaped, roughly one hundred feet long and twenty to thirty feet across. It had two rows of windows on the side facing them, which shone with an intense light. Flames came out of its tail. Both men thought that it was an experimental military aircraft—in Chiles's homely terms, "a new army jet job." Most of the passengers on the flight were asleep, but one, C. L. McKelvie, reported seeing a bright streak of light pass his window. Meanwhile, at Robins Air Force Base near Macon, Georgia, the crew chief on duty spotted a very bright light passing overhead at high speed.

The Chiles-Whitted sighting received ample attention in the media. The Air Force's Project Sign decided after investigating to submit an "Estimate of the Situation" to Air Force Chief of Staff Hoyt Vandenberg, suggesting that the objects seen by Arnold, Mantell, Chiles, and Whitted were extraterrestrial. In public, meanwhile, the authorities insisted that what Chiles and Whitted had seen must have been a meteor. This explanation, which was rejected by many members of the public, helped spread the conviction that the US Air Force knew more than it admitted about UFOs and was engaged in a cover-up.

**SEE ALSO:** The Nash-Fortenberry Sighting (1952), The Flight 1628 Sighting (1986), The Alderney Sighting (2007)

"ESTIMATE OF THE SITUATION": Chiles recorded his impression of the craft in this drawing.

# THE MARIANA FILM

During the twentieth century, minor league baseball was anything but a minor obsession in small towns across the United States. Minor league teams trained future stars for the big leagues and provided lively entertainment for local audiences. That was why Nick Mariana, the general manager of the Great Falls Selectrics, and his secretary, Virginia Rauning, were inspecting the home field at Legion Stadium in Great Falls, Montana, on the morning of August 15, 1950.

Then a bright flash overhead caught their attention. They looked up as two bright disk-shaped objects, roughly 50 feet wide and 150 feet apart, sped through the sky above them. Mariana had a 16 mm movie camera in his car. He sprinted to the vehicle, got out the camera, and shot sixteen seconds of color film before the objects vanished from sight. Mariana had the film developed promptly and showed it several times to local community groups.

That was when the US Air Force intervened. Captain John Brynildsen came to interview Mariana and Rauning, tried to convince them that they had seen light reflecting off two jet fighters, and arranged to take the film to Wright-Patterson Air Force Base for study. When interviewed by a reporter in Great Falls, Brynildsen said he had received eight feet of film from Mariana, but his message to his superiors at Wright-Patterson, since declassified, stated that he had received fifteen feet of film.

When the film came back to Mariana some weeks later, he found that the first thirty-five frames of the film—the ones that showed the disks most clearly—had been removed. The air force denied this, but people who had seen the film before its period in air force custody sided with Mariana. All this helped spread the belief that the air force was perpetrating a cover-up.

**SEE ALSO:** The Ummo Affair (1966), The Gulf Breeze Encounters (1987), The Tic-Tac Incident (2004)

THE MYSTERIOUS MOVING PICTURE: An aerial view of Great Falls, Montana, records the terrain that Mariana captured with his fifteen (or was it eight?) feet of film.

# PROJECT BLUE BOOK

The US Air Force already had a checkered reputation among people interested in UFOs before news of the Mariana film broke. The first air force investigation of UFO phenomena, Project Sign, was launched in late 1947. In the late summer of 1948, it issued an initial report suggesting that the flying saucers were real, that they were not Soviet or American in origin, and that they could be extraterrestrial craft. This report, titled "Estimate of the Situation," was rejected by Air Force Chief of Staff Gen. Hoyt Vandenberg, who shut down Project Sign and replaced it with Project Grudge, tasked with debunking the UFO phenomenon.

By 1952, this had produced so much bad publicity for the air force that Project Grudge was shut down and replaced by yet another program, Project Blue Book, under the direction of Captain Edward J. Ruppelt. In its early days, Project Blue Book engaged in serious investigation of UFO sightings, establishing a standard questionnaire for witnesses and placing a Blue Book officer at every air force base in the country.

In 1953, however, the air force changed its mind. Eight of the ten staff members supporting Ruppelt's work were reassigned, and a new directive (Regulation 200-2) was issued to air force officers to classify all UFO cases with unknown causes and discuss publicly only those that had prosaic explanations. By August of that year, Ruppelt was out of the project. In December, Joint Army-Navy-Air Force Regulation 146 was issued, making it a crime for military personnel to discuss classified UFO reports with any unauthorized person. Thereafter, Project Blue Book served as a venue for debunking, offering dubious explanations that very few people believed. The conviction that the air force was hiding something became more widespread with every year that passed.

SEE ALSO: The Condon Report (1969), Government Hearings on UAPs (2023)

A GOVERNMENT CONSPIRACY?: This photograph taken by Shell R. Albert on July 16, 1952, shows unidentified flying objects in a "V" formation.

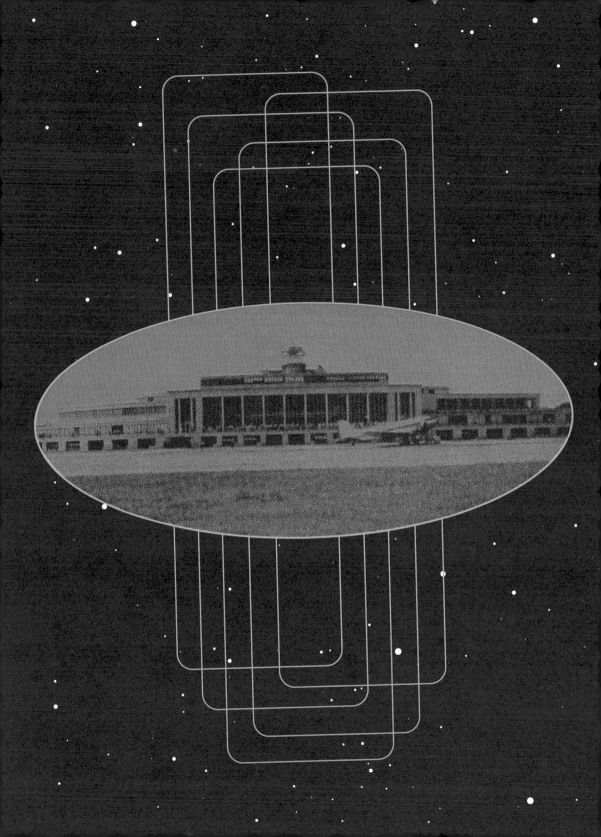

# THE NASH-FORTENBERRY SIGHTING

For all the publicity given to the Mantell and Chiles-Whitted sightings, UFO sightings were sparse after the great 1947 flap. In 1952, however, the saucers came back in force. Between the beginning of April and the end of August in that year, US Air Force investigators logged more than a thousand sightings in the United States alone. Curiously enough, the new wave began just after the air force had reorganized its UFO reporting program, renaming it Project Blue Book, and provided ample material for an article on UFOs in *Life*, one of the most popular magazines of the era. The article was titled "Have We Visitors from Space?" and supported the extraterrestrial hypothesis.

Of the many sightings that followed, the Nash-Fortenberry sighting was among the most famous. On the evening of July 14, 1952, pilot William Nash and copilot William Fortenberry climbed into the cockpit of a Pan Am DC-4 airliner and took off on a routine passenger flight from New York to Miami. Nothing unusual happened until 8:12 p.m., when they were at eight thousand feet above Chesapeake Bay near Norfolk, Virginia. That was when they spotted six glowing red disks in the air below them, off to the southeast, about two thousand feet above the waters of the bay.

As experienced pilots, Nash and Fortenberry were both familiar with aircraft of all kinds and with the optical effects of the atmosphere, and both said they had seen nothing like the disks before. As both men watched, the disks flew northwest at high speed, passing under the DC-4, and then turned sharply to head due west. Two more disks joined them, and the eight disks flew westward until Nash and Fortenberry lost sight of them. Meanwhile, several witnesses in the Norfolk area reported seeing flying disks around the same time.

**SEE ALSO:** The Chiles-Whitted Sighting (1948), The Flight 1628 Sighting (1986), The Alderney Sighting (2007)

MORE THAN A THOUSAND SIGHTINGS: Reports of mysterious objects proliferated around Norfolk, Virginia, in the year 1952.

# UFOS OVER WASHINGTON, DC

The most dramatic of the UFO sightings in the 1952 flap began just five days after the Nash-Fortenberry sighting. At 11:40 p.m. on the night of July 19, 1952, at Washington National Airport in Washington, DC, air traffic controller Edward Nugent called his supervisor Harry Barnes over. Seven unknown objects appeared on radar fifteen miles south-southwest of the airport. Barnes checked with the airport control tower, which also had radar, and found that the two controllers on shift there had also spotted unknown objects—and a bright light hovering above the airfield. As more reports began to come in, including eyewitness accounts from civilians, Barnes contacted the air force, and two F-94 fighter planes were scrambled to investigate. The lights vanished just before the fighters arrived, reappeared after they left, and remained active until just before dawn.

The sightings were splashed all over US news media, but more was to come. A week later, on the night of July 26, radar screens at Washington National Airport and Andrews Air Force Base once again tracked multiple unknown objects on radar. Four fighter planes were scrambled to intercept them. This time two of the pilots spotted glowing lights in the air and tried to pursue them, but the lights outran the jet fighters with ease. The unknown objects continued their antics until sunrise and were observed by many witnesses.

The July 26–27 sightings also sparked a media furor, and the US Air Force did nothing to slow it down by insisting, after a brief investigation, that the lights had been stars and meteors and the radar signals were produced by a temperature inversion. Very few people outside official air force circles found this convincing.

SEE ALSO: The Tehran Sightings (1976), The Manises Incident (1979), The Night of the UFOs (1986), The Tic-Tac Incident (2004)

THERE IT GOES!: This comic, published in 1952, depicts a sighting over the Capitol Building.

# THE FLATWOODS MONSTER

The year 1952 had already had a record number of North American UFO sightings by September 12. About 7:15 that evening, three boys in the small town of Flatwoods, West Virginia, watched a bright light cross the sky and descend into a patch of woods owned by a neighbor. The boys ran home and described what they had seen. Shortly thereafter, the boys, two adults, and two more local boys went to the neighbor's property to investigate.

They pushed through the woods and reached the top of a hill. There they spotted a flashing red light a short distance away. One of the adults, Eugene Lemon, had a flashlight and pointed its beam toward the light, illuminating a vaguely humanoid figure ten feet tall with glowing eyes. It had clawlike hands, and its body seemed to be swathed in black or dark-green cloth. The witnesses disagreed about its head—one said that the head was shaped like the ace of spades, while another believed that the creature's face was framed by a pointed hood.

The creature made a hissing sound and glided toward the witnesses. Lemon screamed and dropped his flashlight, and the whole party turned and ran. They had no further encounters with the monster or anything else uncanny that night.

The "Flatwoods Monster," as the creature was soon dubbed, made news headlines all over the region. Skeptics insisted that the creature had to be a barn owl, though they failed to explain how rural West Virginians had mistaken a familiar species of owl for a ten-foot-tall monster. Few people at the time recalled that humanoid cryptids with glowing eyes had been reported all over the eastern half of North America for centuries, and so the Flatwoods Monster sighting helped feed the burgeoning UFO phenomenon of the 1950s.

**SEE ALSO:** Mothman! (1966), The Rise of High Strangeness (1969), The Ilkley Moor Close Encounter (1987)

AN EERIE TALE: An illustrator created this rendering of the Flatwoods Monster based on the account of the mother of the two boys who witnessed it.

# THE CONTACTEE
# ERA BEGINS

orn in Poland but raised in the United States, George Adamski held many jobs and moved frequently before finding a niche as a teacher of occultism in Los Angeles. His organization offered classes on reincarnation and positive thinking, hosted a radio program, and gathered a circle of students. Some of those students were with him on December 13, 1952, when, following a psychic intuition, he set out for Desert Center, California, in the hopes of contacting a flying saucer.

According to his own account, corroborated by his students, he was successful in his quest. After leaving the car behind and walking alone into the desert, Adamski saw a flying saucer land and met with its occupant. The saucer pilot appeared to be entirely human, with long blond hair. Communicating with Adamski using telepathy, he gave his name as Orthon, claimed to be from Venus, and passed on a warning about the dangers of nuclear weapons.

This was only the first of many encounters with the same blond alien and many others, which were chronicled in three bestselling books. Adamski was not the first person to claim contact with UFO occupants—his friend and fellow occultist George Van Tassel got there first with the 1952 book *I Rode a Flying Saucer*—but he was the first contactee to seize the public imagination and set a pattern that many other contactees followed after him.

Skeptics accused Adamski of faking the photographs he claimed to have taken of the saucers, and scientific UFO researchers did their best to ignore the contactees and focus on less colorful reports of sightings. None of that kept Adamski from having a major impact on public attitudes toward the emerging UFO phenomenon.

**SEE ALSO:** The Giant Rock Convention (1953), World Contact Day (1953), *When Prophecy Fails* (1954), The Billy Meier Contacts (1975), The Heaven's Gate Suicides (1997)

EXTRATERRESTRIAL PHOTOGRAPHER: Professor George Adamski is pictured here at the Temple of Scientific Philosophy in Laguna Beach, California, in 1938, standing alongside his telescope.

# THE GIANT ROCK CONVENTION

On the wake of Adamski's bestselling first book, many other people came to believe that they were in contact with the interplanetary intelligences behind the flying saucers. Adamski's friend George Van Tassel was also among the early figures in the movement. His 1952 book *I Rode a Flying Saucer* attracted some attention, but much more came his way in 1953, when he announced that he was receiving psychic communications from Venus.

Van Tassel had given up a successful career in the aircraft industry in 1947 to live in rooms excavated under Giant Rock, a boulder seven stories tall near Landers, California. That was where he led meditation sessions for students of his College of Universal Wisdom, and it was also where he hosted the annual Giant Rock Spacecraft Convention.

From 1953 until Van Tassel's death in 1978, the convention was the most important gathering of UFO contactees, with up to ten thousand people in attendance. It played a central role in evolving a contactee

subculture and setting the stage for the New Age movement of the late twentieth century. It also gave impetus to Van Tassel's most enduring project, the Integratron.

According to Van Tassel, his alien contacts passed on detailed instructions for building a structure that would prolong human life and open the way to the secrets of antigravity and time travel. Except for a metal shell on the outside, it is made entirely of nonmagnetic materials—wood, concrete, glass, and fiberglass—without a single metal nail or screw. In 1978, with only a few last details remaining to complete the Integratron, Van Tassel went to visit friends in Santa Ana and, while there, suddenly died. The Integratron still exists, but the final details were never written down and it remains permanently unfinished.

**SEE ALSO:** The Contactee Era Begins (1952), World Contact Day (1953), *When Prophecy Fails* (1954), The Billy Meier Contacts (1975), The Heaven's Gate Suicides (1997)

PSYCHIC COMMUNICATIONS FROM VENUS: The Integraton, pictured here, is the round, acoustically perfect chamber built by George Van Tassel for communicating with extraterrestrials.

7

# WORLD CONTACT DAY

California was the epicenter of the North American UFO contactee scene in the early 1950s, but the phenomenon was attracting interest all over the continent by then. The first membership organization for UFO research, the International Flying Saucer Bureau (IFSB), was founded in Bridgeport, Connecticut, in 1952 by pioneering UFO researcher Albert K. Bender. It promptly attracted more than six hundred members and published a quarterly journal, *Space Review*.

In late 1952, the members of the IFSB decided that it was time to try to make contact with the pilots of the mysterious saucers. Like most early UFO groups, the IFSB had a large number of occultists in its membership, and the method they chose to reach the saucers was mass telepathy. On March 15, 1953, beginning at 6:00 p.m. Eastern Time, IFSB members entered into meditation and concentrated on a text that began, "Calling occupants of interplanetary craft!"

The response was not the one Bender hoped for. Even before World Contact Day, Bender claimed that he was being followed by strange men with glowing eyes. According to his later account, three men dressed in black suits visited Bender's home several times and told Bender that he was to shut down the IFSB. In October 1953, Bender mailed one last issue of *Space Review*, closed the organization, and abandoned any further research into UFOs.

World Contact Day ended up having an unexpected echo in popular culture, however. Twenty years later, John Woloschuk of the Canadian progressive-rock band Klaatu read about it and used the message as the lyrics for a 1976 song, "Calling Occupants of Interplanetary Craft." It became one of the band's major hits. A version released a year later by the Carpenters became even more widely played.

**SEE ALSO:** The Contactee Era Begins (1952), The Giant Rock Convention (1953), *When Prophecy Fails* (1954), The Men in Black (1956), The Billy Meier Contacts (1975), The Heaven's Gate Suicides (1997)

CALLING OCCUPANTS OF INTERPLANETARY CRAFT: This advertisement for Gray Barker's *They Knew Too Much About Flying Saucers*, a book about the kind of cover-up that stopped the IFSB, is an example of the cultural resonance prompted by World Contact Day.

# RAdAR

N° 284 - 26 SEPTEMBRE 1954
Canada 15 cents
6 fr. belges-56 fr. 65 suisses
Hebdomadaire
16 PAGES **30** Francs
Maroc (par avion) 40 fr.

# RECONSTITUE LA FANTASMAGORIQUE APPARITION "MARTIENNE" QUI SIDÉRA Marius DEWILDE

*Grâce à ses dessinateurs et reporters photographes, RADAR s'est attaché à reconstruire avec une extrême minutie l'hallucinante apparition dont fut témoin M. Dewilde (ci-dessous) garde-barrière dans le Nord. Événement à peine croyable : il aurait vu atterrir, près de sa maison, une soucoupe volante!*

**H**ALLUCINATION ? Vérité ?

Marius Dewilde, ouvrier métallurgiste à Quarouble (Nord), prétend avoir vu une soucoupe volante, posée sur la voie ferrée qui dessert les Houillères nationales, à 6 mètres de sa maison. De petites créatures, vêtues d'une sorte de scaphandre, coiffées de casques en matière translucide, avaient réintégré en courant, le mystérieux engin. Ayant voulu s'en approcher, Marius Dewilde avait été paralysé par un rayon qui, brutalement, avait jailli de l'appareil.

Trois jours plus tôt, deux cultivateurs d'Acheux-en-Amiénois (Somme), Emile Renard et Yves de Gillate, avaient été les témoins, prétendaient-ils, de l'atterrissage d'une autre soucoupe volante dans un champ, à 200 mètres de la route d'Harponville à Contay. L'appareil oscillait à quelques centimètres du sol.

Enfin, dernière nouvelle (en en attendant d'autres !). Antoine Massud, fermier à Mauriazac (Corrèze), se serait trouvé nez à nez avec un passager d'un « navire spatial » qui lui aurait témoigné des sentiments... pacifiques.

De telles nouvelles — sensationnelles, il faut l'avouer — ne sont pas sans susciter l'incrédulité de beaucoup. Mais pour ceux qui, depuis sept ans, se penchent sur le troublant problème des soucoupes volantes, elles ne font que rééditer certains témoignages recueillis par l'Oursan, un organisme de recherches qui fixe maintenant à sept le nombre de ces « navires de l'espace » ayant atterri sur le territoire français.

Mais la France n'a pas le privilège de ces visites surprenantes.

Le 24 juin 1947, un aviateur américain, Arnold Kenneth, apercevait au-dessus du mont Rainier (Etat de Washington) « 9 objets scintillants évoluant à hauteur des pics neigeux ». Ils ressemblaient à des soucoupes surmontées d'une protubérance qui affectait la forme d'une tasse renversée. Chacun d'eux avait à peu près l'envergure d'un quadrimoteur « C 54 ».

A partir de cette date, il ne se passa pas de semaine sans que des mystérieux engins ne fussent signalés quelque part dans le monde.

L'« U.S. Air-Force », sans prendre tout d'abord position, collecta tous les témoignages et chargea l'A.T.I.C. (Air Technical Intelligence Center) d'ouvrir une enquête. Celle-ci, dénommée « Soucoupe Project », démontra que, sur 270 cas examinés, 60 % pouvaient être expliqués : il s'agissait de ballons-sondes, d'appareils de recherches de rayons cosmiques, de météores, voire d'oiseaux. Mais pour les autres 40 %, le mystère subsistait.

Malgré cette restriction, lorsqu'au mois de décembre 1949, l'enquête « Soucoupe Project » fut close, les conclusions furent que les soucoupes volantes étaient une plaisanterie ; qu'il s'agissait, en fait : ou bien d'objets connus ; ou bien de mystifications ; ou bien d'hystérie collective ».

Cependant, comme le phénomène continuait à se manifester avec une ampleur croissante, l'« U.S. Air-Force » rouvrit « Soucoupe Project » discrètement sous l'appellation neutre de « Project Bluebook » ou « Commission Grudge », ou « Project Sign ».

**SUITE PAGES 2-3**

# THE MARIUS DEWILDE ENCOUNTER

The flying saucer sightings of the late 1940s and early 1950s were concentrated in the United States, but 1954 brought a flurry of sightings in Europe. One of the most striking was the experience of Marius Dewilde, a railway employee in the town of Quarouble in France. At 10:30 on the night of September 10, 1954, he heard his dog begin barking frantically outside. When the barking continued, Dewilde got a flashlight and went outside to investigate.

On the railroad tracks next to his home, some twenty feet away from him, was an object he could not identify. He heard footsteps behind him and turned to find two small humanoid creatures about three feet tall approaching him. Then a beam shot out of the object on the tracks, immobilizing Dewilde. The beings went past him to the object and climbed into a hatch. The object then lifted off and flew away, changing colors as it went. Once the object was gone, Dewilde could move again, and he called the police at once.

Investigation that night and the next day found several unexplained physical traces. Dewilde's flashlight and his telephone, an old-fashioned variety powered by a battery, had stopped working. The gravel under the train tracks where the object had landed was carbonized and had been pressed down over an area nearly twenty feet across. Dewilde himself could not approach the area where the object had been without becoming suddenly sick.

The aftermath, however, provided the strangest and most unsettling evidence. Dewilde's dog, which had previously been in good health, died suddenly a few days after the incident, and three cows in the area were found dead with their bodies inexplicably drained of blood: an example of the cattle mutilation phenomenon that would fill headlines in the United States two decades later.

SEE ALSO: The Straight Line Mystery (1954), The Socorro Landing (1964), The Cattle Mutilation Mystery (1973), The Dechmont Law Close Encounter (1979), The Voronezh Close Encounter (1989)

LA FANTASMAGORIQUE APPARITION: Recorded in the September 26, 1954, edition of *Radar* (with art by Rino Ferrari), Marius Dewilde encounters strange and terrible visitors.

# MYSTERIOUS FLYING OBJECT IN FRANCE

PARIS, Thursday. — Military authorities at Metz, eastern France, are investigating an army report of an object "like a flying Christmas tree decoration."

The object was held for three hours in the beam of a searchlight operated by soldiers at the army stand of a fair. The soldiers said that the object, about 50 metres across, remained stationary at an altitude of about 10,000 metres.

Meanwhile, with other reports in France of flying saucers, flying teacups, flying mushrooms and flying bells, came the story of a 15-year-old boy who said he met a "flying cigar" piloted by a man who spoke to him said the man told him "You can look at it, but don't touch."

# THE STRAIGHT LINE MYSTERY

Marius Dewilde's experience was part of an extraordinary burst of UFO phenomena over France. The sightings began in the early hours of August 23, 1954, when several witnesses in Vernon watched a huge, luminous, cigar-shaped object in the air above their town. One at a time, five glowing disks emerged from the object and flew away. Three weeks later, on September 14, an identical object was sighted by dozens of witnesses in villages on the Atlantic coast more than three hundred miles away, again releasing disks.

In the weeks that followed, glowing disks appeared in various parts of the country, as well as in Germany, Austria, Italy, and Finland. By the end of September, several researchers had already noticed that the disks apparently followed straight line tracks across country, and a sighting in one village would be followed after an interval by a sighting in another along the same trajectory. One object spotted above Rome at 4:45 p.m. on September 17, for example, flew north-west in a straight line and was observed by multiple witnesses above central France, still following the same linear route.

The wave of sightings reached its peak between October 1 and 11, when thousands of witnesses across France observed glowing disks, spheres, and egg-shaped objects crossing the sky, forming one of the busiest UFO waves ever recorded. The media furor was so intense that one French municipality passed a law forbidding UFO overflights of its vineyards, though there is no record of it being enforced.

A few sightings took place in the days that followed, but by late October the wave had ended. French newspapers took the easy way out and mocked the witnesses, but the emerging French UFO research community worked overtime collecting accounts and documenting the remarkable way so many of the unknown objects followed exact great-circle paths through the sky.

**SEE ALSO:** The Marius Dewilde Encounter (1954), The Socorro Landing (1964), The Dechmont Law Close Encounter (1979), The Voronezh Close Encounter (1989)

A BURST OF SIGHTINGS IN FRANCE: A newspaper report from October 1954 mentions a "Flying Christmas Tree"–shaped UFO seen over France.

# THE STADIO ARTEMIO FRANCHI SIGHTING

Whether you call it soccer, as we do in America, or football, as they do everywhere else in the world, the game being played on the afternoon of October 27, 1954, at the Stadio Artemio Franchi in Florence, Italy, was an absorbing spectacle. Two powerhouse Italian soccer clubs, Fiorentina and Pistoiese, were in the middle of play with more than ten thousand avid fans looking on. Then some of the fans noticed something in the air above the stadium. Others looked up as well.

The whole stadium went silent, and then ten thousand voices cried out in astonishment. High overhead was a light-colored object, described variously as egg-shaped and cigar-shaped, moving very slowly. From it came glittering white threads that drifted just as slowly to the ground. The referees stopped the game for ten minutes while players, coaches, and fans alike watched the mysterious object drift past.

They weren't the only ones to see strange things in the sky that afternoon. Witnesses in downtown Florence spotted twenty small, fast-moving shining spheres flying past the dome of the Cathedral of Santa Marie del Fiore. Panicked phone calls to the offices of the *La Nazione* newspaper sent staff members out onto the roof, where they saw the unknown objects.

Adding to the mystery, the fluffy white threads that fell from the craft over the stadium evaporated not long after they reached the ground. Skeptics insisted that these were webs from migrating spiders, but scientists from the Institute of Chemical Analysis at the University of Florence succeeded in obtaining a sample before it dissolved into air. They found that it contained boron, silicon, calcium, and magnesium—and the first two of these are not found in spider silk. The entire sequence of events that day has never been adequately explained.

**SEE ALSO:** The Robozero Sighting (1663), The Boiani Mission Sightings (1959), The Voronezh Close Encounter (1989), The Ariel School Close Encounter (1994), The Tinley Park Sightings (2004), The Stephenville Sightings (2008)

SEEN BY TEN THOUSAND PEOPLE: Gathered to watch a soccer match, a huge audience was in attendance at Stadio Artemi Franchi, pictured here.

# WHEN PROPHECY FAILS

While these sightings were taking place in Europe, much of the action in the American UFO scene focused on the contactee subculture. Hundreds of people claimed to speak with alien intelligences, and many thousands of others believed them and listened to their teachings. Some produced impressive bodies of philosophy and teaching. Then there was Dorothy Martin.

Martin was the trance medium at the heart of a circle of UFO believers in East Lansing, Michigan. She believed she was receiving telepathic messages from the Guardians, a group of aliens from the planet Clarion, who had an apocalyptic warning to pass on to humanity. According to Martin, the Guardians announced that a tremendous earthquake and tidal wave would destroy the United States on December 21, 1954, and only those who were taken away aboard flying saucers would survive.

This announcement came to the notice of a team of sociologists from the University of Minnesota headed by Leon Festinger, and several researchers infiltrated Martin's group to observe what happened when the end of the world failed to happen. The result was one of the great classic books of American sociology, *When Prophecy Fails*, which was published in 1956. Festinger and his associates used pseudonyms for Martin and her followers, but this did little to reduce the embarrassment of the group.

Afterward, Martin went to Peru, where she took part in an unsuccessful attempt to found a religious center in the Andes. Returning to the United States, she took the name Sister Thedra, settled in Mount Shasta, California, and continued channeling messages from the aliens for a mostly uninterested world. Later on, she relocated to the New Age mecca of Sedona, Arizona, where she died in 1992.

SEE ALSO: *The Book of the Damned* (1919), The Contactee Era Begins (1952), The Giant Rock Convention (1953), World Contact Day (1953), *Chariots of the Gods?* (1968), The Billy Meier Contacts (1975), *Communion* (1987), *Behold a Pale Horse* (1991), The Heaven's Gate Suicides (1997)

CONTACTEE CULTURE: One of the greatest works of sociology was written after a study involving the infiltration of a circle of UFO believers.

# AREA 51

"One of the most desolate regions on the face of the earth." That was Lieutenant George Montague Wheeler's description of the area around Groom Lake in southern Nevada, which he explored for the US Army in 1869 and 1871. The word "lake" makes the area sound more hospitable than it is; a dry lake bed dotted with sagebrush, inhabited by six different species of rattlesnakes, Groom Lake is among the most barren corners of the Nevada desert.

That was what attracted Kelly Johnson of Lockheed's "Skunk Works" secret facility to the area. In the spring of 1955, Johnson chose Groom Lake as the perfect test site for the top-secret U-2 spy plane, the Skunk Works' latest project. Hangars, a long runway, and mobile homes went in, and the U-2s began their first flights. The airspace above the base and the desert landscape around it were put off-limits to anyone but authorized personnel. For security reasons, the base was given a variety of labels: to Lockheed employees it was Paradise Ranch; the contractors who built it called it Watertown Strip; air traffic controllers referred to it as Dreamland. On government maps it got the bland label Area 51.

The U-2 was far from the only secret plane to find a home at the Groom Lake base. The SR-71 Blackbird and a flotilla of prototype stealth planes first took wing there. According to well-documented claims, so did at least two planes that officially don't exist, the SR-91 Aurora and the TR-3 Black Manta. As interest in UFOs picked up throughout American society, rumors spread that flying craft of nonhuman origin had also been seen in the airspace around Groom Lake. Decades after the U-2 was declassified, these rumors would become a lightning rod for troubling claims about the US government's relationship with the UFO phenomenon.

**SEE ALSO:** The Paul Bennewitz Affair (1982), The Majestic-12 Papers (1984), John Lear and UFO Conspiracy (1987), The Bob Lazar Disclosures (1989), The Planet Serpo Papers (2005)

ENTRANCE TO A SECRET FACILITY: This gate in front of the fabled Area 51 at the United States Air Force Nellis Testing Range in Lincoln County, Nevada, warns potential visitors to stay out.

# NATIONAL INVESTIGATIONS COMMITTEE
## ON AERIAL PHENOMENA
### WASHINGTON 6, D. C.

TELEPHONE NORTH 7-9434

CABLE ADDRESS:
SKYLIGHT

ADMINISTRATIVE OFFICES:
1536 CONNECTICUT AVE., N.W.

April 3, 1957

Dear friend:

Your interest in our investigation of Unidentified Flying Objects (flying saucers) is greatly appreciated. Since 1950 the Air Force has kept thousands of authentic UFO reports from the public. While we believe we know their reasons, we are convinced that Americans have a right to the truth. To that end, NICAP has set up a nationwide network—soon to be worldwide—for reporting UFO sightings and hidden developments.

All this information — uncensored — will be revealed to NICAP members in a monthly magazine and in confidential bulletins. The magazine will include dramatic, authentic sightings by veteran pilots and other competent witnesses; behind-the-scene stories of the Air Force secret investigation; proof of the censorship which has muzzled hundreds of pilots; the pro's and con's of the question, "Is there life on Mars?"; and special articles on the UFO problem and our own space-travel plans.

In addition, NICAP will hold public hearings on claims of contacts with spacemen—to expose hoaxes and also to ferret out the facts. All this will be covered in the monthly magazine, with many other features, such as— a serialized history of UFO's with new sidelights on famous sightings; frank answers to readers' questions; and a monthly department in which I shall reveal some "inside stories" I have learned in the last two years.

As an Associate Member of NICAP—for an annual fee of $7.50—you will receive the monthly magazine and the special bulletins. You will also be priviledged to join a NiCAP club in your area and become part of our large reporting network. Most important of all, you will be playing a vital role—not only in aiding to end the censorship—but in helping to find all the answers to the UFO mystery.

To become a NICAP member, merely forward your $7.50 membership fee to

NICAP
1536 Connecticut Avenue
Washington 6, D. C.

We hope you will join us in this factual yet fascinating work.

Sincerely yours,

Donald E. Keyhoe, Major USMC (Ret.)
Director of NICAP

DEK:RHC

*A privately-supported fact-finding body serving the national public interest.*

# NICAP INVESTIGATES THE PHENOMENON

By 1956, the air force's efforts to debunk UFO sightings had become blatant and clumsy enough that even within the US military and intelligence community, many people had become convinced that something genuinely strange was being covered up. Once Project Blue Book stopped investigating UFO sightings, the idea of founding a civilian research organization to do the same thing was on many minds. Two such organizations, Alfred K. Bender's short-lived International Flying Saucer Bureau (IFSB) and Coral Lorenzen's more successful Aerial Phenomena Research Organization (APRO), pioneered that option, but the most influential group of the kind was the National Investigations Committee on Aerial Phenomena (NICAP), founded on October 24, 1956, by a group of civilian scientists and high-ranking retired military officials.

Under the leadership of Major Donald Keyhoe, who became director in 1957, NICAP pursued a two-pronged strategy. The first prong involved recruiting associates all over the United States to carry out thorough field investigations of UFO sightings. The second involved lobbying Congress to hold public hearings on the UFO evidence. At its peak in the early 1960s, NICAP had more than fourteen thousand members and published one of the classic works on UFOs, *The UFO Evidence*, which summarized hundreds of unexplained sightings.

In the wake of the 1968 Condon Report, however, Keyhoe was forced to resign by the board of governors; several members of which subsequently turned out to have close links to the CIA. The new management shut down the local and state affiliate groups and suspended all further investigations of UFO sightings. Few members stayed long after that, and the organization shut down forever in 1980.

**SEE ALSO:** Coral Lorenzen's First Sighting (1934)

A REPORT ON UNEXPLAINED SIGHTINGS: At one point, the National Investigations Committee on Aerial Phenomena (NICAP) had over fourteen thousand members.

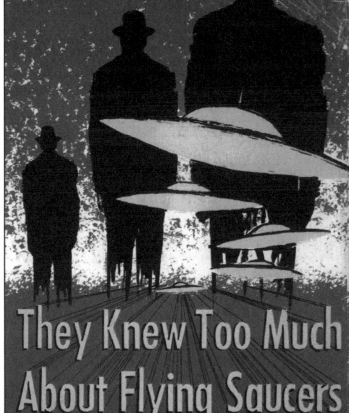

# They Knew Too Much About Flying Saucers

## GRAY BARKER

THE TRUE STORY OF WHAT HAPPENED TO CERTAIN RESEARCHERS AND
INVESTIGATORS WHO FOUND OUT WHERE THE SAUCERS COME FROM

# THE MEN IN BLACK

Longtime UFO writer Gray Barker was an anomaly in a field full of true believers and humorless skeptics. While he doubted most stories of the paranormal, he was fascinated with them and was not above adding lurid details to make a good story or even engaging in outright hoaxing if an opportunity arose. A native of West Virginia, he heard about the Flatwoods Monster when it was still a local news story and became a regular author for Albert K. Bender's *Space Review* before Bender abruptly closed it down.

Bender's story of three men in black suits who ordered him to stop investigating flying saucers intrigued Barker, who knew of several other stories of seemingly official figures showing up to warn witnesses not to talk about UFOs. In 1956, he used these stories as the basis for a lively and lurid book, *They Knew Too Much About Flying Saucers*, which launched the idea of the Men in Black into the collective imagination of the UFO research community.

According to Barker, the Men in Black traveled in groups of three, wore black suits, and drove big black cars, usually Cadillacs. They showed up without warning and tried to intimidate witnesses and researchers alike into silence concerning UFO activities. A later book coauthored by Barker and Albert K. Bender, *Flying Saucers and the Three Men*, argued that there was good reason for this—the Men in Black were themselves extraterrestrials.

Barker apparently meant all this as a joke, but it took on an unexpected seriousness in the years that followed as UFO witnesses encountered Men in Black identical to the ones in Barker's book. Whether the US Air Force or some other government agency chose to play along with Barker's joke for reasons of their own, or something even stranger was going on, remains an open question.

**SEE ALSO:** World Contact Day (1953), Mothman! (1966), The Rise of High Strangeness (1969)

THEY KNEW TOO MUCH!: Gray Barker's classic text stoked the fires of suspicion in government agents employed to intimidate those who reported sightings.

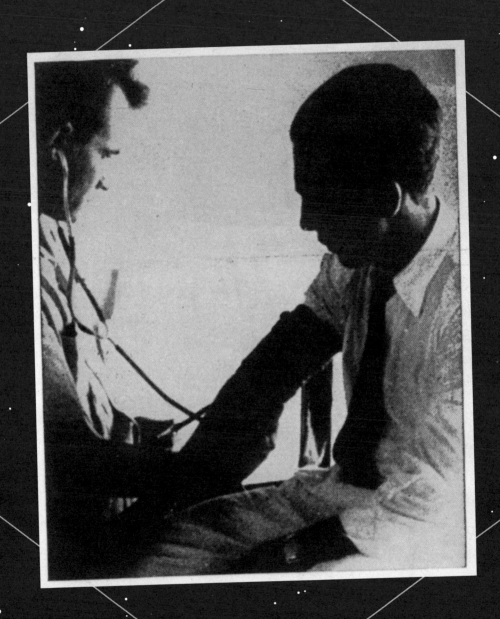

# THE VILAS-BOAS
# ABDUCTION

Antônio Vilas-Boas was a Brazilian farmer who lived near São Francisco de Sales in the state of Minas Gerais, Brazil. Like most farmers in the region, he worked at night to avoid the daytime heat. That was why he was out plowing on the night of October 15, 1957, when he noticed a red light high in the sky. The light descended, and after a few minutes he saw that it was an egg-shaped craft, which extended three landing legs and settled on the ground. Vilas-Boas panicked and tried to drive away on his tractor, but its engine and lights died.

He tried to flee on foot but was seized and wrestled to the ground by four humanoid beings five feet tall, wearing gray coveralls and helmets, who spoke in barking or yelping sounds. They dragged him into their craft, stripped him, coated his skin with a gel, took a blood sample, and exposed him to a gas that made him ill. Then another of the beings came into the room: a female, entirely nude, who seduced him. After they finished, she smiled at him, rubbed her belly, and pointed at the sky.

He was then given back his clothing, shown around the ship, and returned to the tractor, where he stood watching as it took off again and vanished in the night sky. Over the days that followed, he suffered from nausea and weakness. When his story came to the attention of UFO researchers, he was examined by a medical expert, Dr. Olavo Fontes, who concluded that Vilas-Boas was suffering from mild radiation sickness.

The Vilas-Boas encounter was one of the first abductions to receive wide publicity in the UFO literature, and it was also one of the first reported cases of sexual contact between UFO occupants and humans. Both of these became much more common in the years that followed.

SEE ALSO: The Barney and Betty Hill Abduction (1961), The Hickson-Parker Abduction (1973), The Emilcin Abduction (1978), The Zanfretta Encounter (1978), The Knowles Family Encounter (1988), The Cahill Abduction (1993)

VISITORS FROM AN EGG-SHAPED CRAFT: Brazilian farmer Antônio Vilas-Boas, abducted while working at night, is given a medical examination by investigators in this photo from 1957.

# THE BOIANI MISSION SIGHTINGS

Papua New Guinea is very far away from the regions most haunted by UFOs in the 1950s, but one of the decade's most dramatic sightings happened there. At 6:02 p.m. on June 26, 1959, Father William Gill, an Anglican missionary then living in Boiani on the north coast of Papua New Guinea, noticed a bright white light in the northwestern sky above the sea. Since it seemed to be approaching the mission, Gill called to others to come see. A crowd of thirty-eight people assembled outside the mission and watched the object approach.

Gill and the other witnesses described it as a large, brightly lit disk-shaped object with four legs extending from beneath and four windows on the side facing the viewers. It flew about three hundred feet above the sea and gradually came to a halt in midair. At intervals, a shaft of blue light shot up from the disk at an angle into the clouds overhead. Then four apparently human figures came out onto the upper surface of the disk and busied themselves doing something. After twenty-five minutes, the object rose up into the clouds overhead and was lost to sight.

At 6:00 p.m. the next day, astonishingly, the same sequence of events happened. This time, Gill and one of the other witnesses waved their arms—and the figures on the top of the disk waved back. Gill called for them to land, but after a little while the figures went back inside the craft. It remained hovering for more than an hour, but then heavy clouds rolled in and the object was lost to sight. It did not appear again.

Gill's report of his sighting caused a media furor in Australia and led to questions in the Australian Parliament. The Royal Australian Air Force carried out a pro forma investigation and then insisted that Gill and the other witnesses had seen the planets Jupiter, Saturn, and Mars.

**SEE ALSO:** The Robozero Sighting (1663), The Stadio Artemio Franchi Sighting (1954), The Westall School Sighting (1966), The Voronezh Close Encounter (1989), The Ariel School Close Encounter (1994), The Tinley Park Sightings (2004)

SUNSET OVER PAPUA NEW GUINEA: Although this island nation hasn't recorded many incidences of possible contact, the Boiani mission sightings earned it a place in the pantheon of locations where extraterrestrials may have visited.

Copied 22 July 1960 from 8x10" print rec'd
23 May 1960 from ATIC, Wright-Patterson AFB,
Ohio thru SAF-OI

(over)

# THE CRESSY CIGAR

With the 1960s, the UFO phenomenon spread worldwide, and Australia received a good share of important sightings thereafter. Tasmania, the big triangular island off the southeastern end of the Australian mainland, was a particular hot spot. One of the most remarkable and best known of the many sightings there was the "Cressy Cigar."

Cressy is a small farm town in north central Tasmania. About 6:10 on the evening of October 4, 1960, the local Church of England minister, Rev. Lionel Browning, and his wife were in their home watching a rainbow to the east. Mrs. Browning drew her husband's attention to a cigar-shaped object about one hundred feet long that had just emerged from the clouds. A dull metallic gray in color, it had what appeared to be antennas protruding from its front end. It moved north at sixty to seventy miles an hour, staying about four hundred feet above the ground.

After the object had been in sight for approximately one minute, it stopped, and six small saucer-shaped objects that appeared to be made of shiny metal came out of the clouds and stationed themselves around it at a distance of half a mile. A few seconds later, the cigar and the saucers flew southward and, after another minute, vanished into the clouds again. Neither of the two witnesses noticed any unusual sounds during the period of the sighting.

Rev. Browning called in the sighting to the control tower at Launceston, the nearest airport, and later gave a detailed account to the local paper. UFO researchers in Tasmania and elsewhere interviewed both the Brownings. So did officers of the Royal Australian Air Force (RAAF), who duly issued a report insisting that the Brownings had seen moonlight reflecting off a cloud. Neither the Brownings nor anyone who knew them considered this likely.

**SEE ALSO:** The Exeter Incident (1965), The Westall School Sighting (1966), The Alderney Sighting (2007)

METEOROLOGY OR MORE?: A collection of photos from 1960 identifies (from top left) lenticular clouds, noctilucent clouds, parhelia phenomena, and a mirage, all of which are commonly mistaken as "flying saucers."

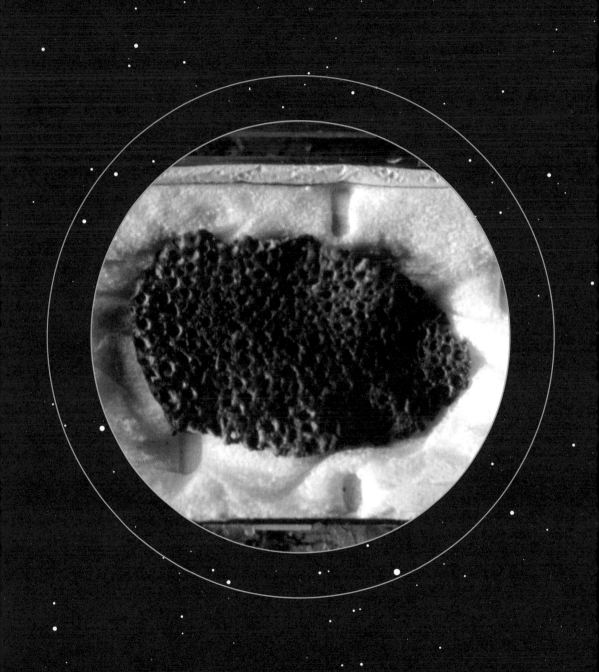

# PANCAKES FROM SPACE?

Alongside the more routine types of UFO encounters—the lights or disks sighted in the sky, the brief close encounters with beings associated with a landed craft—there are others hard to fit into any familiar category. These "high strangeness" cases came to play an increasingly important role in the UFO experience in the 1960s. One of the strangest occurred to Joe Simonton, who reported that he was given three pancakes cooked aboard a flying saucer.

Simonton was a sixty-year-old chicken farmer who lived near Eagle River, Wisconsin. About 11:00 a.m. on April 18, 1961, he heard a peculiar noise from outside and went to look. In his yard, hovering just above the ground, was a silvery disk twelve feet high and thirty feet across. A hatch opened in the saucer, revealing three occupants. About five feet tall, they had dark skin and hair and wore garments with turtleneck tops and knit helmets.

One of them held up a jug and motioned to Simonton to fill it. The baffled farmer took the jug indoors, filled it with water, and returned it. When he returned, he saw that one of the men appeared to be frying pancakes on a grill. In return for the water, Simonton was handed three of the pancakes, each about three inches in diameter and perforated with small holes. Then the hatch closed, the craft rose up noiselessly twenty feet or so, and flew off to the south.

The local sheriff and UFO investigator J. Allen Hynek both reported that Simonton clearly believed in the truth of his experience. One of the pancakes was analyzed at a US government lab at the request of the air force. It was made of ordinary earthly ingredients—wheat, buckwheat, soy, and hydrogenated fat—but contained no salt: an odd parallel with traditional fairy lore, which claims that food associated with fairies always lacks salt.

SEE ALSO: Voyagers from Magonia (815), The Cussac Close Encounter (1967), The Rise of High Strangeness (1969)

IHOP (INTERSTELLAR HOUSE OF PANCAKES): Was this tasty breakfast treat a gift from extraterrestrial visitors?

New Hampshire UFO Chiller

# THE BARNEY AND BETTY HILL ABDUCTION

US Highway 3 runs down the mountainous middle of New Hampshire. That's where Barney and Betty Hill were on the night of September 19, 1961, as they returned from a vacation in Canada to their home in Portsmouth, New Hampshire. Around 10:30 p.m., a little south of Lancaster, New Hampshire, they both spotted a bright point of light in the sky moving against the background of the stars. They stopped for a while at a picnic area, then drove on. The light appeared to move toward them, becoming a glowing disk with windows. Finally, it hovered above the road ahead of them.

Barney, who was driving, stopped the car and got out. He saw humanoid figures through the windows. Then, as far as he could remember, he got back in the car and drove on. The Hills got home at dawn, three hours later than they expected. Their watches had stopped working and their clothes and shoes were scuffed. Then Betty began having strange dreams about being captured and examined by gray-skinned humanoids, and the two of them sought medical help.

When they were hypnotized by medical hypnotist Benjamin Simon, a weird story came out. Both the Hills described being made to drive off the highway into the forest and then stopped and taken aboard a flying saucer, where they underwent medical examinations. Their stories were mostly consistent with each other, though details varied. Betty also recalled being shown a diagram she interpreted as a star map; an investigator, Marjorie Fish, proposed that the map traced the visitors to the double star system Zeta Reticuli, about thirty-nine light-years from Earth.

This has been challenged by skeptics, as has almost every other detail of the case. Nonetheless, the Barney and Betty Hill encounter has become the most famous of all UFO abduction cases and played a potent role in shaping the UFO narrative.

SEE ALSO: The Vilas-Boas Abduction (1957), The Hickson-Parker Abduction (1973), The Emilcin Abduction (1978), The Zanfretta Encounter (1978), The Knowles Family Encounter (1988), The Cahill Abduction (1993)

THE ZETA RETICULI INCIDENT: Betty and Barney Hill (pictured here with an article about the event) recorded an abduction that became the basis for many future UFO narratives.

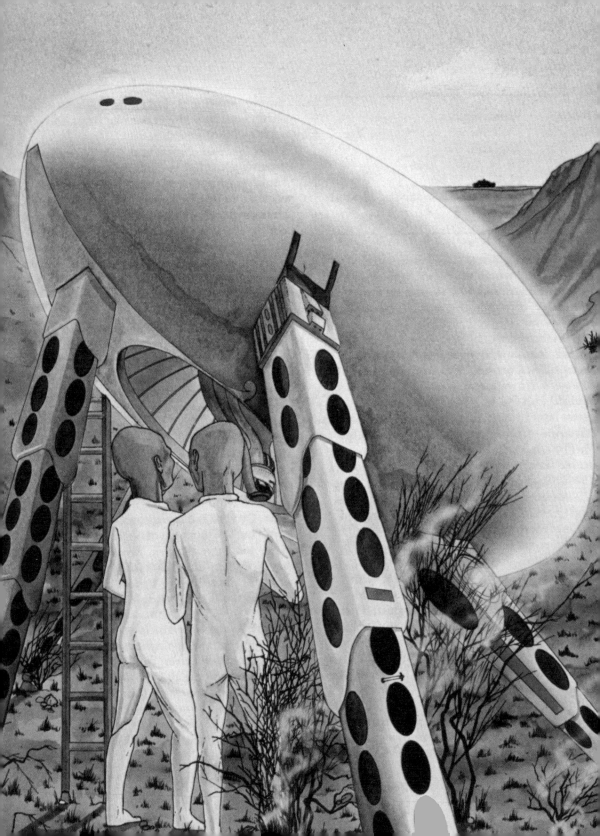

# THE SOCORRO LANDING

Dionicio "Lonnie" Zamora was an officer in the Socorro, New Mexico, police department. Around 5:45 p.m. on April 24, 1964, he was chasing a speeding car south of Socorro when he heard a roar and saw a flame some distance off the road. Concerned that a local dynamite shack might have exploded, he broke off the pursuit and drove toward the site of the apparent explosion, calling the police dispatcher for backup.

A glint of sunlight on metal caught his attention and he drove through it, thinking first that it was an upturned car and then that it was a half-deflated weather balloon. When he came closer, he saw that it was an egg-shaped metallic object the color of aluminum resting on the ground on four extensible legs. Two figures in white coveralls were standing near the object but climbed into it as Zamora approached. He then heard a roaring sound and saw a blue and orange flame from beneath the object, which rose into the air and moved away at high speed. Other police officers arrived shortly thereafter. When they reached the scene, they found brush and grass smoldering where Zamora said the object had taken off.

The apparent landing was investigated by UFO researchers and also by officers from the US Air Force's Project Blue Book, which listed the cause of the sighting as "unknown." US media covered it extensively. One skeptic, Steuart Campbell, may have earned the prize for the most absurd attempt at an explanation by insisting that the sighting was "almost certainly" a mirage of the star Canopus (which of course is not visible in daylight). A less improbable theory that circulated among UFO researchers suggested that Zamora witnessed the test of some variety of secret US craft from the White Sands Missile Range not far away. The Socorro encounter nonetheless remains unsolved to this day.

**SEE ALSO:** The Marius Dewilde Encounter (1954), The Straight Line Mystery (1954), The Dechmont Law Close Encounter (1979), The Voronezh Close Encounter (1989)

A GLINT OF SUNLIGHT ON METAL: The Socorro encounter, depicted in this illustration, remains unsolved to this day.

# THE EXETER INCIDENT

One of the best documented and most highly publicized of all UFO sightings, the Exeter sightings began early on the morning of September 3, 1965. Eighteen-year-old Norman Muscarello was walking to his home in Exeter, New Hampshire, after a visit to his girlfriend in a neighboring town. He was a few miles outside Exeter on Route 150 when he noticed five flashing red lights up ahead. When he came closer, he realized that they were mounted on a dark saucer-like shape between eighty and ninety feet across, hovering in the air above the trees near two farmhouses. After a while it moved over one house then went into a nearby wooded area.

Panicking, Muscarello flagged down a car and was driven to the police station in Exeter. A police officer on duty, Eugene Bertrand, had already interviewed another witness who had seen the same craft earlier that night. Bertrand took Muscarello back to the scene. When they left the police car and walked toward the wooded area, the same object rose up from among the trees. Bertrand called for backup and another officer, David Hunt, came to the scene and witnessed the same craft. All three witnesses watched as the craft rose out of sight. Several other witnesses reported similar flying objects to the police that same night.

The sighting got national publicity from the US news media and became the subject of a famous book, *Incident at Exeter* by John Fuller, which made the *New York Times* bestseller list. Skeptics and air force officials insisted that the witnesses must have seen aircraft flying from nearby Pease Air Force Base, but the witnesses were familiar with air force flights from that base and insisted that what they had seen was entirely different. The resulting controversy did nothing to dissuade believers in an air force cover-up.

**SEE ALSO:** The Cressy Cigar (1960), The Swamp Gas Incident (1966), The Cash-Landrum Encounter (1980), The Stephenville Sightings (2008)

**INCIDENT AT EXETER:** Norman Muscarello's story of alien abduction, pictured in this illustration, was the basis for a bestselling book.

# THE KECKSBURG CRASH

The evening of December 9, 1965, turned unexpectedly dramatic in Michigan and Ontario at 4:43 p.m., when a brilliant fireball shot out of the northeastern sky above Detroit and Windsor, two towns separated by a national border and a river. Hundreds of witnesses, including twenty-three aircraft pilots, watched the fireball as it crossed the heavens, heading southwest. Witnesses in Pittsburgh a few minutes later reported a sonic boom. In the town of Kecksburg, Pennsylvania, thirty miles south of Pittsburgh, local people watched an object plunge from the sky into the nearby woods, while others heard the impact.

Local residents went to investigate and reported seeing an acorn-shaped object the size of a small car, with markings on the outside that resembled hieroglyphics. Shortly thereafter, the crash site was sealed off by state police officers, and air force personnel arrived to investigate the scene. The next day, authorities insisted that nothing had been found at the site, but Kecksburg resident John Hays said he watched a military flatbed truck leaving the area with a car-sized object covered with tarpaulins.

The official story issued by government offices for the next four decades was that the fireball had been an ordinary meteor and the Kecksburg crash never happened at all. In 2005, however, officials at NASA released a statement claiming that metallic fragments recovered from the Kecksburg site proved that a Russian satellite had crashed there—but that all NASA records on the subject had somehow been lost. Further investigations and Freedom of Information Act requests have yet to turn up any more information. Outside the inner circles of the US government, the Kecksburg crash remains a mystery.

**SEE ALSO:** The Aurora Crash (1897), The Tunguska Event (1908), The Roswell Crash (1947), The Shag Harbour Crash (1967), The Rendlesham Forest Landing (1980), The Megaplatanos Crash (1990), The Varginha Close Encounters (1996)

THE SPACE ACORN: Pictured here, this massive sculpture is actually a facsimile of the original unidentified object, created for the TV show *Unsolved Mysteries* and then left in Kecksburg, Pennsylvania, for visitors to enjoy.

# THE TULLY CROP CIRCLES

The town of Tully is located in the far north of Australia's Queensland state. Not far away, next to the smaller town of Euramo, is an area called Horseshoe Lagoon. That's where George Pedley was on the morning of January 19, 1966, driving a tractor, when he heard a hissing sound. Thinking that one of the tires had been punctured, he stopped the tractor. Just then, a disk-shaped object some thirty feet across rose from amid the reeds and trees of a nearby wetland, flew a short distance, and vanished in a puff of blue vapor.

Once he got over his shock at this unexpected sight, Pedley went to investigate and found that in the place where the object had been, the reeds were flattened in a perfect circle, forming a clockwise swirl. Later that day he brought the property owner, Albert Pennisi, to see the site. Pennisi waded out into the swamp and found that the reeds had not just been flattened—they had been torn up by the roots and formed into a matted circular mass. Pennisi and Pedley also found a rectangular area near the circle where another set of reeds had simply vanished.

As word spread, sightseers began to gather, and other farmers in the area began searching their property. Five more "nests" were discovered. Reporters came to investigate, and so did officers from the Royal Australian Air Force, who insisted that the "nests" must have been the result of some natural phenomenon, such as a whirlwind. Other researchers determined that other "nests" had in fact been found in the area for several years, but their cause was unknown to the local farmers. All this got ample attention among UFO investigators, but its real significance was not understood until similar circles began appearing in grain fields on the other side of the world—the first wave of England's crop circles.

**SEE ALSO:** The Mowing Devil (1678), The Circle Makers Unveiled (1991)

MYSTERY OF THE CROP CIRCLES: Indelibly associated with extraterrestrial craft, crop circles have long been attributed to natural phenomena, but questions remain.

# THE WESTALL SCHOOL SIGHTING

Westall School was an ordinary Australian school in Clayton South, a suburb of Melbourne. Around 11:00 on the morning of April 6, 1966, some three hundred schoolchildren were out for their morning recess under the supervision of several teachers. The ordinary noises of a school playground fell suddenly silent as a disk-shaped craft, gray or silvery, came into sight. The witnesses estimated that it was about twice the size of a family car. The object was silent as it descended slowly into a nearby meadow behind a screen of pine trees.

Twenty minutes later, the same object rose up from the meadow and flew northwest at a high speed until it could no longer be seen. While it was still visible, five unmarked aircraft came flying after it and followed it out of sight. Some of the schoolchildren ran toward the meadow, where they found a ring of flattened grass where the object had been seen.

Once the children returned from recess, the headmaster of the school told them not to talk about what they had seen or they would be punished. According to other reports, men in business suits went around Clayton South in the days following the sighting, cautioning people not to mention the sighting. The next day's newspaper featured an article claiming that the object had been a weather balloon—a claim few of the witnesses accepted.

A further wrinkle emerged in 2005, when researcher Keith Basterfield uncovered records of secret balloon flights used to monitor British nuclear testing at Maralinga in the Australian Outback. If a balloon from that program had been blown off course, it might have come down in the meadow in Clayton South and then gone up again. This proposal remains an unproven hypothesis, however.

SEE ALSO: The Stadio Artemio Franchi Sighting (1954), The Boiani Mission Sightings (1959), The Swamp Gas Incident (1966), The Voronezh Close Encounter (1989), The Ariel School Close Encounter (1994), The Tinley Park Sightings (2004)

UP IN THE SKY: In this photograph of the Westall UFO encounter, an unexplained flying object hovers in the air before descending into a nearby open field.

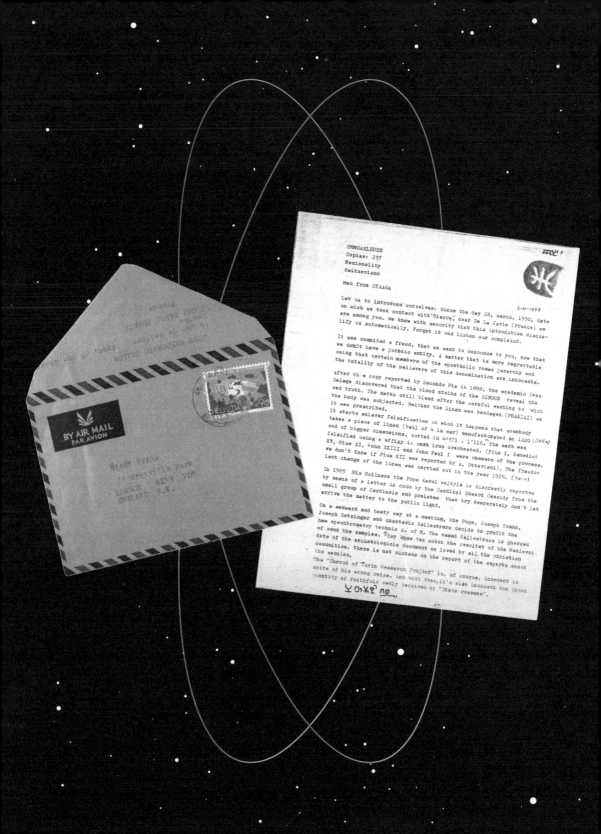

# THE UMMO AFFAIR

The letters started showing up in mailboxes in Spain and France in 1966. Clumsily typed and marked with the curious emblem )+(, they had been mailed from around the world to scientists and UFO researchers. They claimed to come from humanlike aliens living secretly on Earth. Their planet was named Ummo; it circled the star Iumma, 14.6 light-years from Earth, which Earthling scientists call Wolf 424; they had detected Earth via our radio signals, and their expedition landed on Earth near the French town of Digne on March 28, 1950. The letters contained avant-garde scientific concepts and information about Ummo's culture and history.

This caused an understandable stir among UFO researchers and scientists in Europe. Interest reached fever pitch when an apparent close encounter took place near Madrid on June 1, 1967, which included marks on the ground, odd artifacts, and clear photos of a saucer-shaped craft with the Ummo emblem on the bottom. Close analysis of the photos, however, proved that they were clever fakes, and the artifacts turned out to have earthly origins.

Most researchers classified the Ummo affair as a hoax thereafter, but it was not until 1992 that the details came out. That was when Spanish psychologist José Luis Jordan Peña admitted that he had launched the hoax himself with the help of a friend who took the letters to distant locations to be mailed. He had also faked the photos and the landing. Behind it all, as UFO researcher Jacques Vallée had surmised years before, was a famous 1940 story by Argentine writer José Luis Borges, "Tlön, Uqbar, Orbis Tertius," which described how a similar prank had spun out of control and reshaped our world in its image. Peña's creation didn't have quite so world-shaking an effect, but it left a significant mark in the world of UFO research.

**SEE ALSO:** The Mariana Film (1950), The Gulf Breeze Encounters (1987), The Tic-Tac Incident (2004)

LETTERS FROM UMMO: These handwritten letters arrived via snail mail, purporting to be from aliens living incognito on Earth.

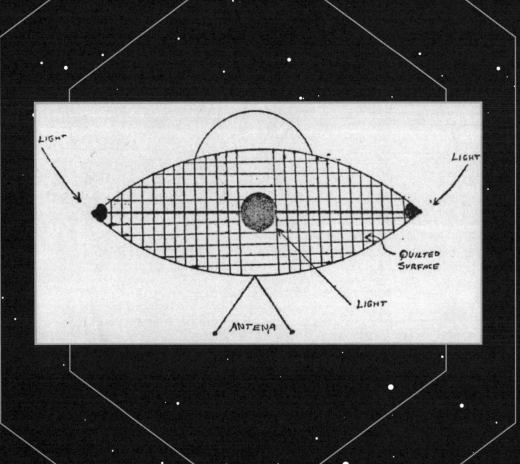

# THE SWAMP GAS INCIDENT

The furor began with phone calls to police departments in western Michigan in the early hours of March 14, 1966. Residents across the region reported seeing glowing disks, red and green, moving at high speed through the sky. Several police officers saw the disks themselves. The objects vanished before sunrise, but on March 17 they returned for a repeat performance.

March 20 brought an even more dramatic event. A local farmer, Frank Mannor, saw a bright light outside. When he and his son Ron went to look, they found themselves staring up at a disk-shaped object the size of a car, with a flat bottom, a domed top, and brilliant lights. As they watched, it blinked out of sight, reappeared some distance away, repeated this process, and then flew away at high speed. Two police officers called by Mannor also witnessed the object.

The next night the same thing happened at Hillsdale County College. Seventeen young women in a dormitory watched a similar object appear and reappear then hover close to the ground. Local police and civil defense officials came in response to their phone calls and also witnessed the strange object.

All in all, it was an ordinary mid-1960s UFO sighting, but the air force response turned it into a media circus. They sent astronomer J. Allen Hynek to investigate, who suggested that the Mannor sightings might have resulted from methane gas seeping from a nearby marsh. The air force and the national media promptly insisted that the entire incident had been explained as swamp gas. This was too much for the public to swallow and led to a huge outcry. It also inspired the congressman from that district, Gerald R. Ford, to hold hearings in the House of Representatives. Out of these would come the Condon Committee fiasco.

**SEE ALSO:** Project Blue Book (1952), The Westall School Sighting (1966), The Condon Report (1969), The Ariel School Close Encounter (1994), Government Hearings on UAPs (2023)

DRAWINGS OF A VISITATION: Numerous individuals around western Michigan recorded their brushes with these strange disklike craft.

# MOTHMAN!

Weird events began to cluster around Point Pleasant, West Virginia, in the autumn of 1966. Mysterious lights moved through the night sky or hovered over outlying houses. Travelers on lonely roads reported flying objects zooming overhead during daylight hours or landing to disgorge grinning, humanlike beings who asked strange questions and told stranger stories. Meanwhile, Men in Black showed up without warning to confront witnesses and warn them not to tell anyone about their experiences. For over a year it was a three-ring circus of weirdness.

The weirdest of all these sightings clustered around the "TNT area," an abandoned munitions plant from the Second World War. That was where witnesses spotted a huge gray winged figure with blazing red eyes. People in the area started calling the entity "Mothman." Skeptics insisted the creature must be a sandhill crane, but witnesses shown pictures of a sandhill crane insisted that the bird did not resemble the entity they had seen.

As scores of UFO researchers converged on the area and sightings continued to pour in, rumors began to spread through the Point Pleasant community, claiming that something terrible was about to happen. Those rumors were confirmed by sudden tragedy when the Silver Bridge across the Ohio River at Point Pleasant collapsed under rush-hour traffic on December 15, 1967, plunging dozens of cars and trucks into the frigid water. Thirty-eight people died in the disaster. Afterward the strange events stopped, never to resume. Point Pleasant today remains a mecca for people interested in the unexplained, and the bizarre events of 1966 and 1967 played an important role in forcing UFO researchers to confront the stranger side of the phenomenon.

**SEE ALSO:** The Flatwoods Monster (1952), The Men in Black (1956), The Rise of High Strangeness (1969), The Ilkley Moor Close Encounter (1987)

MOTHMAN STRIKES!: This gleaming metallic statue welcomes visitors to Point Pleasant, West Virginia, where a Mothman festival is held once a year.

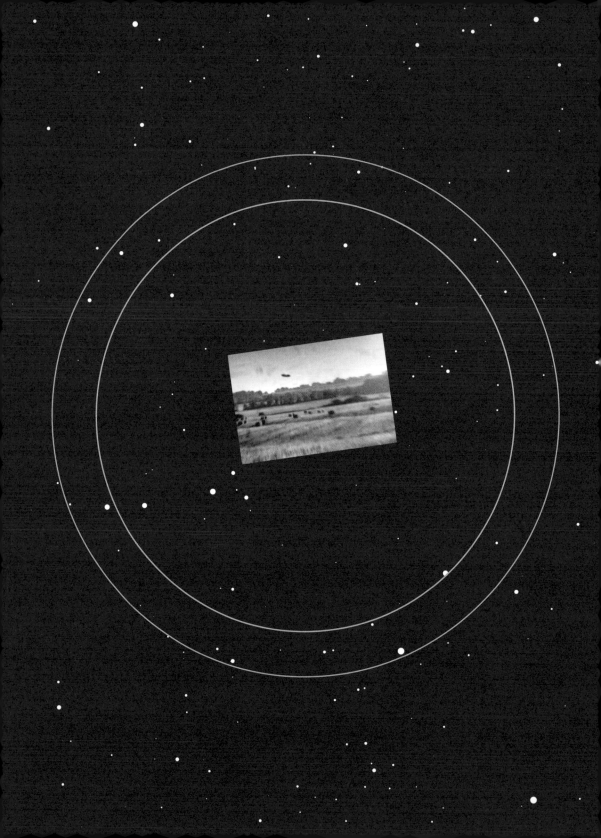

# THE CUSSAC CLOSE
# ENCOUNTER

The late 1960s saw a massive wave of UFO sightings and close encounters in Europe as well as the US. One of the most famous sightings of that period took place near Cussac on the Cantal Plateau, Auvergne, France, on August 29, 1967. Around 10:30 a.m., a thirteen-year-old boy, François Despleches, and his nine-year-old sister, Anne-Marie, were tending cows in their family's pastures that day with their dog Medor. François suddenly spotted four entities a little over three feet tall. The entities were forty feet away from them; they and their clothing were completely black and seemed to have a silken texture. Near them was a shining silvery sphere around six feet across.

François called out to the entities, thinking that they were children. The entities, seeing that they had been spotted, rose up one by one into the air and dove through the top of the sphere, which then rose with a hissing sound, circled over the field, and flew off to the northwest, leaving a sulfurous scent behind. At this point the cows started bellowing and Medor barked and tried to chase the sphere; the children called the dog back, herded the cows home, and then reported what they had seen.

Researchers from GEPAN, the French institute for UFO research, interviewed the children and discovered that they could still smell the sulfur in the dry grass where the sphere had been. This seems to have communicated nothing to the investigators, but anyone familiar with rural French folklore could have identified the creatures at once. For many centuries, French rural people have told stories about elf-like creatures called *lutins* or *farfadets*, which can fly through the air and are associated with the smell of brimstone. Sightings of this kind helped give credibility to alternative views of the nature of UFOs in the decade that followed.

SEE ALSO: Voyagers from Magonia (815), Pancakes from Space? (1961), The Rise of High Strangeness (1969)

A SIGHTING IN RURAL FRANCE: This blurry photograph is one example of a UFO caught over a scene of pastoral tranquility.

# THE SHAG HARBOUR CRASH

It was an ordinary evening on Air Canada flight 305, en route to Toronto on October 4, 1967, until 7:15 p.m. That was when First Officer Robert Ralph sighted a shining rectangular object followed by a string of smaller lights a few miles off the left side of the aircraft. He brought it to the attention of Captain Pierre Charbonneau. As the two men watched, an explosion shook the object. A second blast followed before the plane flew out of sight of the object.

That same evening, off Sambro, Nova Scotia, Captain Leo Mersey of the fishing vessel MV *Nickerson* observed an anomaly on his ship's radar. He and the entire crew of the *Nickerson* went on deck and watched four lights in a rectangular formation crossing the northeastern sky seventeen miles away. Many other witnesses on the southern coast of Nova Scotia saw the same object and reported it to local newspapers and the Royal Canadian Mounted Police (RCMP).

Around 11:20 p.m., according to witnesses, a brightly lit low-flying object hurtled across the sky with a whistling sound and struck the water off Shag Harbour, Nova Scotia. Several people saw the object, still illuminated, floating in the sea. Thinking that an airplane had crashed, witnesses called the RCMP, which sent two officers to the harbor at once. When they arrived, the object was still visible in the water but had begun to sink. Local fishing boats went out at once to look for survivors. By the time they reached the scene, the object had vanished from sight. Neither they nor a later coast guard search found any debris, bodies, or survivors.

Meanwhile, local authorities had determined that no known aircraft flight had disappeared anywhere in the Maritime Provinces or New England. Divers sent to the sea floor found no trace of anything unusual. The cause of the Shag Harbour incident remains unknown.

SEE ALSO: The Aurora Crash (1897), The Tunguska Event (1908), The Roswell Crash (1947), The Kecksburg Crash (1965), The Megaplatanos Crash (1990), The Varginha Close Encounters (1996)

FISHERMAN FROM BEYOND THE STARS: This lobster-alien statue marks a historic UFO crash site in Nova Scotia.

# CHARIOTS OF THE GODS?

The idea that extraterrestrials may have visited the earth in ancient times had been raised already by other writers before Erich von Däniken's bestselling book *Chariots of the Gods?* saw print in 1968. Harold T. Wilkins and Robert Charroux both penned nonfiction works on that theme. So, to his later embarrassment, did Carl Sagan, whose 1966 book *Intelligent Life in the Universe* (coauthored with Soviet astrophysicist Iosif Shlovskii) made cogent arguments for the possibility that the myths of ancient peoples might include records of extraterrestrial visitors.

It was von Däniken's book, however, that launched the ancient astronaut hypothesis into public awareness. A hotel manager with a checkered past, including convictions for theft and fraud, von Däniken was an unlikely figure to launch so dramatic a cultural shift. His arguments were sometimes weak and his facts fairly often garbled or simply wrong, but *Chariots of the Gods?* and its many sequels were enormously successful. In an era when sightings of mysterious flying craft were common and the official explanations for those sightings failed to satisfy many people, many readers were willing to consider the possibility that such craft had been sighted by people in antiquity and the official explanations for human history were wrong.

*Chariots of the Gods?* had another important impact on the UFO controversy. In its wake, barriers rose between the mainstream scientific community and alternative researchers. Carl Sagan's career traces that process exactly: the same man who was theorizing about ancient astronauts in 1966 contributed to a heavily marketed volume denouncing Däniken ten years later. Sagan went on to become one of the main public faces of the backlash against alternative culture that drove the rise of the skeptic movement in the years that followed.

**SEE ALSO:** Mysterious Visitors (5000 BCE), *The Book of the Damned* (1919), *When Prophecy Fails* (1954), *Communion* (1987), *Behold a Pale Horse* (1991)

A GIFT FROM ANCIENT ALIENS?: Some believe that these Easter Island Moai heads are physical evidence of a prehistoric visitation.

# THE CONDON REPORT

On April 5, 1966, a congressional subcommittee convened by Representative Gerald Ford grilled Air Force Secretary Harold Brown about the US Air Force treatment of the UFO phenomenon. In response, the air force set out to find a university willing to take over the study of UFOs. After some searching, a team at the University of Colorado headed by physicist Edward Condon was selected and began work in the autumn of 1966.

Civilian UFO research groups cooperated with the Condon Committee at first, turning over reams of data collected by their members. Their hope that the committee would study the phenomenon impartially was soon dashed, however, when Condon gave a speech in January 1967 in which he dismissed UFOs as nonsense, commenting with a smile, "but I'm not supposed to reach that conclusion for another year." In July, a memo from Condon Committee member Robert Low got into the media, explaining that the entire project was intended as a debunking exercise. Low wrote: "Our study would be conducted almost exclusively by nonbelievers who, although they couldn't possibly prove a negative result, could and probably would add an impressive body of evidence that there is no reality to the observations."

The final report of the Condon Committee was just as negative as the Low memo suggested. Published in 1969 as *A Scientific Study of Unidentified Flying Objects*, it insisted that there was nothing to be gained by further research into UFOs, even though nearly a third of the sightings included in the study were still unexplained. To the scientific mainstream, it became a justification for the blanket dismissal of UFOs; among UFO researchers, it reinforced the conviction that the political and military establishments were engaged in a cover-up.

**SEE ALSO:** Project Blue Book (1948), The Swamp Gas Incident (1966), Government Hearings on UAPs (2023)

"NO REALITY TO THE OBSERVATIONS": Physicist Edward Condon, pictured here, was part of a team tasked with studying UFOs.

# THE RISE OF HIGH STRANGENESS

Until the fiasco of the Condon Committee, UFO researchers in the United States and many other countries were caught in an awkward dilemma. For most of them, the goal that mattered was getting governments, universities, and the general population to take the phenomenon seriously. One major difficulty they faced was that the phenomenon itself refused to limit its behavior to evidence that would further that goal. Psychic experiences, Men in Black, and even weirder things kept intruding into UFO sightings. Civilian research organizations such as NICAP and APRO thus engaged in self-censorship, ignoring "high strangeness" data and refusing to investigate cases that seemed too likely to bring ridicule on the phenomena.

The aftermath of the Condon Report, however, convinced many UFO researchers that their efforts to make UFOs respectable had been a waste of time. In response, while NICAP and APRO continued to avoid the weirder cases, avant-garde researchers started writing about the high strangeness end of ufology. The most influential of these were Jacques Vallée and John Keel. Vallée's *Passport to Magonia*, published in 1969, explored the parallels between UFO sightings and medieval fairy lore, while Keel's *Operation Trojan Horse*, published the following year, discussed the paranormal events that so often surrounded UFO encounters.

Both Vallée and Keel argued against the extraterrestrial origin of UFOs, pointing out all the evidence showing that the phenomenon has been present here on Earth for millennia or longer. During the decade that followed, speculations about other dimensions and paranormal factors played a much more central role in discussions of UFOs than they had before.

**SEE ALSO:** Voyagers from Magonia (815), The Flatwoods Monster (1952), Pancakes from Space? (1961), Mothman! (1966), The Cussac Close Encounter (1967), The Ilkley Moor Close Encounter (1987)

GET WEIRD: At the end of the 1960s, a school of thought followed that ufology as a scientific study was a waste of time, and that it was useless to fixate on empirical evidence.

# THE HICKSON-PARKER ABDUCTION

The evening of October 11, 1973, was perfect weather for fishing on the shores of the Pascagoula River in Mississippi. That was where local residents Charles Hickson and Calvin Parker were around 9:00 p.m., sitting on a pier on the river's west bank with their fishing lines in the water, when both men suddenly heard a whirring or whizzing sound behind them. Startled, they turned around to discover a glowing, egg-shaped object hovering just above the ground some thirty feet away. They estimated it was thirty to forty feet across and eight to ten feet high, and glowed blue on the side facing them.

As the two men stared, a door opened in the side of the object and three strange beings emerged from it. According to the men, the beings were around five feet tall, with bullet-shaped heads, no necks, slit-like mouths, and thin conical objects projecting in place of eyes and ears. The creatures had gray, wrinkled skin, round feet, and clawlike hands. To their dismay, Hickson and Parker found that they could not move or speak as the creatures floated through the air toward them. At that point, Parker fainted from terror, while Hickson remained conscious as he and his friend were taken into a brightly lit room inside the object, subjected to medical examinations, and then returned to the riverbank.

Terrified, the two men called the local air force base, which referred them to the local sheriff. The sheriff didn't believe them at first, but the men stuck to their story, even when they were put in a supposedly private room and secretly taped. Both men also passed polygraph examinations. Their case is still considered one of the best-documented UFO abduction accounts.

**SEE ALSO:** The Vilas-Boas Abduction (1957), The Barney and Betty Hill Abduction (1961), The Emilcin Abduction (1978), The Zanfretta Encounter (1978), The Knowles Family Encounter (1988), The Cahill Abduction (1993)

ON THE BANKS OF THE PASCAGOULA: Two unassuming fishermen were the subjects of what many believe is one of the best-documented visitation cases.

# THE CATTLE
# MUTILATION MYSTERY

Mysterious deaths of livestock have been taking place around the world for a very long time. Old volumes of strange occurrences record many examples, some going back centuries, and Charles Fort included many examples from Britain in his books of weird happenings. The first connection between these gruesome events and UFOs took place in 1967, when the death of Snippy, a horse in Alamosa, Colorado, made the media. It was not until 1973, however, that cattle mutilation became a major theme of the unfolding UFO phenomenon.

On December 4 of that year, law enforcement officials in Kansas and Nebraska reported a wave of cattle deaths across eleven counties in those states. Thirty-eight animals in all were killed and mutilated. The animals appeared to have been drained of blood and had their sexual organs removed. Some were found in odd circumstances—for example, lying in a field with no tracks leading to the corpse, as though they had been dropped from the air.

The mutilations continued into the following year. Some witnesses reported that unidentified black helicopters were seen hovering, shining spotlights into fields where mutilated cattle were later found. Others reported unidentified objects in the air doing the same thing. More cases occurred each year that followed, and a mass media panic resulted.

Beginning in 1979, a government investigation headed by FBI agent Kenneth Rommel looked into the claims, issuing a report in 1980 insisting that the cattle had all died naturally and that the claims of high strangeness surrounding the mutilations were overblown. This explanation was rejected by many local ranchers as well as by citizen investigators. Mutilated cattle are still found from time to time in North and South America as well as Australian— one more mystery that may or may not be connected to UFOs.

**SEE ALSO:** The Book of the Damned (1919), The Marius Dewilde Encounter (1954), The Rise of High Strangeness (1969)

MOO!: Although the official report was that all mutilated cattle had died of natural causes, many believe otherwise.

# THE BILLY MEIER CONTACTS

While the great UFO boom of the 1970s included many new features, the phenomenon continued many of its older habits as well, and a bumper crop of contactees along the lines of George Adamski were among these. Perhaps the most colorful of the contactees of the 1970s was Eduard "Billy" Meier. Born in Switzerland, he had a troubled youth, spent time in prison for a series of minor offenses, and lost his left arm in a bus accident in Turkey in his late twenties. The nickname "Billy" came from an American friend who likened him to Billy the Kid.

According to Meier, his contacts with alien intelligences began in 1942, when he was five years old. In that year he was befriended by an elderly humanoid alien from the Pleiades named Sfath. Other contacts followed until 1964, when they stopped for a time. In 1975, Semjase, the granddaughter of Sfath, began a new cycle of contacts and started passing spiritual teachings onto him. A Pleiadian man, Ptaah, began interacting with Meier shortly thereafter, and other aliens followed. None of this was accidental, according to Meier's account, because his soul had previously been incarnated as a series of great prophets, including Moses and Jesus.

Meier backed up his claims with photos of saucer-shaped Pleiadian beamships and pictures of some of his Pleiadian contacts. Skeptics argue that the saucer photos are models and the Pleiadians are minor Hollywood actresses photographed from TV shows. None of this stopped Meier from finding an eager audience for his stories and spiritual teachings. His organization, the Free Community of Interests for Borderland and Spiritual Sciences and Ufological Studies, is based in Switzerland and has an international clientele, and numerous books and a movie have recounted his stories of alien contact.

SEE ALSO: The Contactee Era Begins (1952), The Giant Rock Convention (1953), World Contact Day (1953), *When Prophecy Fails* (1954), The Heaven's Gate Suicides (1997)

A FRIEND OF THE PLEIADEANS?: Eduard "Billy" Meier, UFO expert, is pictured here in a photograph from 1976.

# THE TEHRAN SIGHTINGS

On the early hours of September 19, 1976, four people in Tehran, the capital of Iran, reported seeing a bright object in the sky. The Iranian air force sent up an F-4 fighter jet to investigate. Lieutenant Yaddi Nazeri, the pilot of the plane, spotted the object and flew toward it, but when he got within engagement range, all his instruments and communications gear suddenly stopped working. He veered away, and the equipment came on again.

When he returned to base to report, another F-4 was sent up, with squadron commander Major Parviz Jafari at the controls. He described the object as diamond-shaped, outlined in red, green, orange, and blue lights so brilliant that he could not make out its body. He estimated that it was the same size as a Boeing KC-135 Stratotanker. Twenty-seven miles from the target, his radar locked on it, but at that moment the communications gear on Jafari's plane shut down.

Moments later, a bright sphere came from the object and approached Jafari's plane at high speed. Jafari tried to launch a missile at the object, but his weapons control panel shut down. The sphere went past Jafari's plane and he veered away from the object. When his communications came back on, he was ordered back to base. As he left the area, he watched the original object send another bright sphere down to the ground, where it produced a brilliant flash. Residents of the area reported seeing the flash during the night.

The Iranian government, then a US ally, forwarded a report to the US military, and it has since been declassified. Debunkers insisted that the experienced pilots involved in the incident had seen the planet Jupiter, and the communications and armament failures happened at the same time by sheer coincidence. Understandably, few people found this convincing.

**SEE ALSO:** UFOs Over Washington, DC (1952), The Manises Incident (1979), The Night of the UFOs (1986), The Tic-Tac Incident (2004)

JAFARI'S CHASE: Major Parviz Jafari was sent up to pursue an unidentified object.

# THE EMILCIN ABDUCTION

Jan Wolski was an ordinary farmer, seventy years old, who lived and worked in the village of Emilcin in Poland. On the morning of May 10, 1978, he was driving a horse-drawn cart outside the village when two humanoid beings in grayish-black outfits jumped on board the cart. The beings were about five feet tall and had green skin, high cheekbones, and slanted eyes. They spoke to each other in a language unknown to Wolski, directing him with gestures to drive to a clearing in the forest nearby.

There, the astonished farmer saw a white object the size of a bus hovering about sixteen feet above the ground. A platform descended from the craft, and Wolski was motioned onto it and taken aboard. The interior of the craft was the same grayish-black color as the costumes of the beings, and it had no lights inside other than the daylight that came through the door.

Once Wolski was inside, the entities gestured for him to remove his clothes, and they then examined him using an instrument that looked like two saucers side by side. They then motioned for him to dress, offering him something that looked like an icicle to eat, which he refused.

Finally the beings returned Wolski to his cart. He drove home as quickly as he could and told his family what had happened. He and a crowd of family members and neighbors returned to the clearing. There they found the craft gone, but the grass was flattened in all directions, as if it had been trampled. Investigators later found that a local boy had seen something that looked like a bus hovering over a nearby barn and then rising into the sky. Later still, in 2005, a memorial was built in the clearing to commemorate Poland's most famous UFO sighting.

SEE ALSO: The Vilas-Boas Abduction (1957), The Barney and Betty Hill Abduction (1961), The Hickson-Parker Abduction (1973), The Zanfretta Encounter (1978), The Knowles Family Encounter (1988), The Cahill Abduction (1993)

THE MOST FAMOUS POLISH ABDUCTION: The Emilcin UFO memorial, pictured here, consists of a metal cube balanced on a rock.

# THE VALENTICH DISAPPEARANCE

Frederick Valentich was an Australian pilot. At twenty years old, he was still in training as a member of the Royal Australian Air Force Air Training Corps but had 150 hours of flying time and had already earned a class-four instrument rating, qualifying him for night flights. On the evening of October 21, 1978, he took off from Moorabbin Airport near Melbourne in a Cessna 182L airplane, intending to fly from there to Cape Otway and then across Bass Strait to King Island—a total distance of around 125 miles.

At 7:06 p.m., he radioed Melbourne air traffic control to tell them that he was being followed by an unidentified aircraft a thousand feet above him. He did not recognize the type of plane but said it had four bright landing lights. The air traffic controller told him there was no known traffic at that level. Valentich then reported that the other aircraft was approaching his plane and seemed to be deliberately toying with him; he also reported unexplained engine trouble. He said that the aircraft had a shiny metal surface and a bright green light underneath. The last words received by air traffic control in Melbourne was "It's not an aircraft." An unidentified noise described as "metallic, scraping sounds" followed, and then all contact was lost.

An immediate search involving ships and military and civilian aircraft scoured Bass Strait for the next five days but found no trace of Valentich or his plane. Five years later, an engine cowl flap that might have come from the Cessna washed up on Flinders Island, far to the east. Nothing more was ever heard of Frederick Valentich. UFO researchers and skeptics have proposed various explanations for his disappearance, but no conclusive evidence has yet turned up and the case remains unsolved.

**SEE ALSO:** The Mantell Incident (1948)

VANISHED WITHOUT A TRACE: Pilot Frederick Valentich, pictured here, was last heard from during a flight from Melbourne.

# THE ZANFRETTA ENCOUNTER

Pier Zanfretta was a twenty-six-year-old night watchman in the town of Torriglia near Genoa, Italy. On the bitterly cold night of December 6, 1978, he was in his car on the way to an unoccupied house he was tasked with guarding. As he neared the house, the engine, radio, and lights of his car all suddenly died, and he spotted four lights moving in the yard of the house. He got out of the car, got out his revolver and a flashlight, and went to investigate.

Suddenly something touched him on the shoulder. He spun around and found himself staring at a green creature ten feet tall with huge yellow eyes. That was too much for Zanfretta, who turned and ran. Behind him, a huge glowing triangular shape rose up from behind the house, while other creatures like the first came after him and tried to seize him. When he reached the car, the radio was working again, and he called the security company that employed him. The radio operator testified later that Zanfretta was confused and incoherent. When the operator tried to get Zanfretta to describe the "men" who were pursuing him, Zanfretta burst out: "No, they aren't men, they aren't men—" Then the radio went silent.

Another patrol was sent at once. When they arrived, they found Zanfretta lying on the ground in front of the house in a state of shock. The authorities were called, and they found two horseshoe-shaped markings in the snow, nine feet across, near where Zanfretta had seen the glowing object rise. Investigators also found fifty-two people in Torriglia who had seen a bright object near the house where the encounter took place. Zanfretta was examined by doctors and found to be stressed but entirely sane. Unnervingly, he went on to have ten more abduction experiences over the next three years. His experience remains one of the most remarkable UFO abduction cases on record.

SEE ALSO: The Vilas-Boas Abduction (1957), The Barney and Betty Hill Abduction (1961), The Hickson-Parker Abduction (1973), The Emilcin Abduction (1978), The Knowles Family Encounter (1988), The Cahill Abduction (1993)

AN ENCOUNTER IN LIGURIA: The woods of Torriglia, Liguria, may have housed a visitor from beyond our planet.

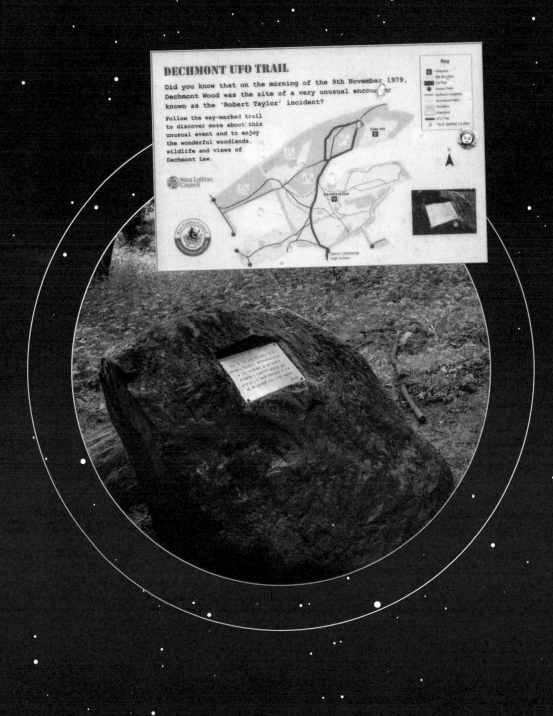

# THE DECHMONT LAW CLOSE ENCOUNTER

Mary Taylor was horrified. On November 9, 1979, her husband, Bob, had driven up to Dechmont Law in West Lothian, Scotland, a nearby hill surrounded by forest, to take their dog, Lara, for a walk. When she next saw him later that same day, he was at their front door, his clothes muddy and torn and his face and thighs scraped and bloody. A "spaceship thing," he said, had attacked him. Mary went to the phone at once and called the police and the family doctor. Over the next few hours, an unnerving story came to light.

Bob Taylor had driven his pickup to a trailhead on the side of a road near the M8 motorway and started up the trail with his dog. Less than a quarter mile on, he encountered a dome-shaped metallic object about twenty-one feet in diameter hovering in a forest clearing. It was surrounded by a smell like burning brakes and by two small metallic spheres that reminded Taylor of sea mines. Several of the spheres went for Taylor and started dragging him toward the larger object. A "powerful gas" came from the dome, and Taylor fainted. When he regained consciousness, the objects were gone and he was sprawled on the ground. His truck would not start, and so he walked back home.

Given Taylor's condition, the local police treated the incident as a criminal assault and investigated. At the site of the encounter, they found odd ladder-shaped marks impressed into the ground, as though an object weighing several tons had rested there. No trace of any such object being driven into or out of the clearing was found. No reasonable explanation of the events of that afternoon was ever offered, and the Dechmont Law encounter remains the only UFO encounter on record that was the subject of a criminal investigation.

SEE ALSO: The Marius Dewilde Encounter (1954), The Straight Line Mystery (1954), The Socorro Landing (1964), The Voronezh Close Encounter (1989)

SOMETHING STRANGE HAPPENED HERE: The Dechmont UFO trail is a twenty to thirty minute leisurely stroll, marked by this plaque commemorating the 1979 encounter.

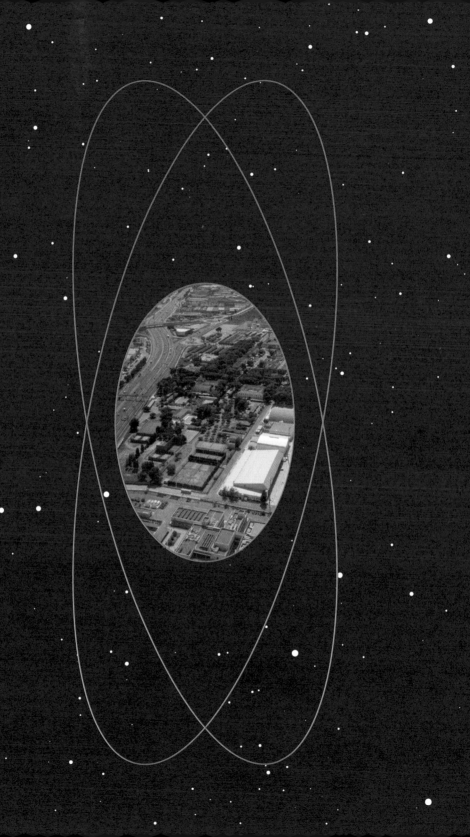

# THE MANISES INCIDENT

On the night of November 11, 1979, TAE (Transportes Aéreos Españoles) Flight JK-297 was on its way from Salzburg, Austria, to Las Palmas, Spain, with 109 passengers on board and pilot Francisco Javier Lerdo de Tejada at the controls. The flight was routine until 11:00 p.m., when the crew observed a set of red lights that appeared to be approaching the aircraft on a collision course. The pilot contacted air traffic control in Barcelona, but neither it nor the military radar at Torrejón de Ardoz was able to identify the source of the lights.

To avoid a collision, Lerdo de Tejada changed altitude. The lights moved along with the plane but stopped approaching and remained about a third of a mile away. At this point, the pilot made an emergency landing at the Manises airport in Valencia, Spain. The lights broke off their pursuit as soon as the plane began to descend, but three other objects were picked up on airport radar and observed by ground crew at the airport.

The Spanish air force scrambled a Mirage fighter jet to investigate. Captain Fernando Cámara, the pilot, spotted an object that he described as a brightly lit cone that changed color, but he had to accelerate to Mach 1.4 to get close to the object, and once he did, it sped up and shot away faster than his plane would fly. He then turned to approach a second object, but this time the plane's electronics suddenly malfunctioned. A third attempt failed to get close to the object, and Cámara returned to base. Spanish officials later claimed that everyone involved had misidentified flares from a distant chemical factory and an assortment of stars and planets—an explanation that none of the people present at the incident accepted.

**SEE ALSO:** UFOs Over Washington, DC (1952), The Tehran Sightings (1976), The Night of the UFOs (1986), The Tic-Tac Incident (2004)

A COLLISION COURSE WITH . . . WHAT?: After the incident, the pilot of Flight JK-297 made an emergency landing at the Manises airport in Valencia.

# THE RENDLESHAM FOREST LANDING

Rendlesham Forest is a wooded area in Suffolk, England, not far from the North Sea. It borders on two military air bases, RAF Woodbridge on the west side of the forest and RAF Bentwaters to the north. In 1980, both bases were occupied by the United States Air Force. At three in the morning on December 26 of that year, a security patrol at the east gate of the Woodbridge air base saw lights descending into Rendlesham Forest. Thinking that they were witnessing an airplane crash, a team of servicemen hurried to the site.

Instead of a crashed airplane, they encountered a large triangular object that glowed with a brilliant white light, illuminating the entire forest. As they approached the object, it moved away through the trees, while livestock at a farm nearby went into a frenzy. The men hurried back to base. In daylight they went back to the site, where they found burn marks and broken branches on the trees and three impressions on the ground, possible marks of landing gear.

On December 28, Lieutenant Colonel Charles Halt, deputy commander of the Woodbridge base, went to the site with an investigative team. A radiation survey meter found increased radioactivity in the area of the apparent landing and also in another small area half a mile away. When night fell, Halt and his men saw "red sunlike light" radiating from the landing site. The light then broke apart into five white objects and vanished.

This much is agreed on by most sources. Many other claims have been made about what might have taken place on that night in Rendlesham Forest. This case has been called "Britain's Roswell," and like the Roswell crash, it has become the focus of many competing narratives and contradictory claims of fact in UFO and skeptic literature.

**SEE ALSO:** The Aurora Crash (1897), The Tunguska Event (1908), The Roswell Crash (1947), The Kecksburg Crash (1965), The Shag Harbour Crash (1967), The Megaplatanos Crash (1990), The Varginha Close Encounters (1996)

LIFE-SIZED REPLICA: The Rendlesham forest UFO trail is marked by this model based on what the USAF personnel claimed to have seen.

# THE CASH-LANDRUM ENCOUNTER

When Betty Cash first saw the light, she thought it was just another airliner coming in to land at Houston International Airport thirty-five miles away and gave it no further thought. She was driving home to Dayton, Texas, with her friend Vickie Landrum and Landrum's grandson Colby. It was around 8:30 on the night of December 29, 1980.

A few minutes later, all three of the car's occupants realized that the object was nothing they recognized. It was a gray, diamond-shaped metallic object many times larger than the car, with a flattened top and bottom and a ring of intense blue lights around the middle. At intervals, flames shot out of the bottom of the object and sprayed down onto the roadway. The object bobbed up and down, rising when the flames came out and sinking after they stopped.

Cash stopped the car and all three of them got out to stare at it. Landrum, a devout Christian, thought at first that the Second Coming was taking place and Christ would shortly appear out of the glowing object. Her grandson, terrified, begged her to come back into the car and after a little while she did so. Cash stayed out watching the vehicle for some minutes. When she returned to the car, the door handle was so hot she had to wrap her hand in her coat to avoid being burnt. She drove on once the object had moved away, and she and the others watched as a small fleet of helicopters—twenty-three in all—came after the object and escorted it as it flew on.

In the hours that followed, all three of the witnesses suffered from nausea, vomiting, and redness and blistering on skin that had been exposed to the object. Cash's symptoms were so serious she had to be hospitalized. Local military officials denied any knowledge—but several other witnesses saw the massed helicopters that same night.

**SEE ALSO:** The Stephenville Sightings (2008)

THE SECOND COMING?: Vickie Landrum talks about the UFO she, her then-7-year-old grandson, and a friend, Betty Cash, encountered in 1980 as they were returning from a bingo game in Dayton, Texas.

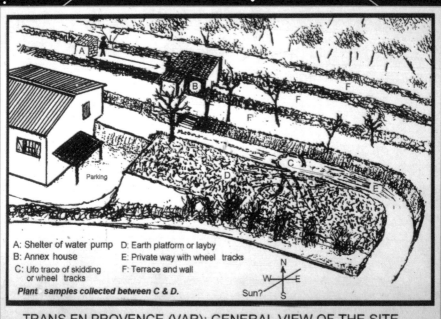

A: Shelter of water pump
B: Annex house
C: Ufo trace of skidding
   or wheel tracks
*Plant samples collected between C & D.*

D: Earth platform or layby
E: Private way with wheel tracks
F: Terrace and wall

Parking

Sun?

TRANS EN PROVENCE (VAR): GENERAL VIEW OF THE SITE

# THE TRANS-EN-PROVENCE LANDING

January 8, 1981, began as an ordinary working day for Renato Nicolaï, a fifty-five-year-old farmer in the town of Trans-en-Provence in southern France. Around 5:00 p.m., however, he heard an unusual whistling noise and spotted a saucer-shaped metallic object landing in a field downhill from the place where he was standing, around 150 feet away from him. He estimated that it was around eight feet in diameter and about five feet thick. The object lifted off almost as soon as it touched down and flew away to the northeast, leaving apparent burn marks on the ground.

So far, this was a UFO case like dozens of others that took place all over the world during the 1970s and 1980s. What set it apart, however, was the thoroughness of the investigation that followed. The day after the sighting, Nicolaï went to the local gendarmerie, who interviewed the farmer, took photos of the site, and gathered soil samples from the field where the saucer touched down. GEPAN, the French government office tasked with investigating UFOs, got involved in the case at once.

Researchers found that the soil where the saucer had landed had been compressed by a weight of four to five tons and heated to a temperature between 600° and 1,000°F. Unexpected traces of phosphate and zinc were found in the soil, and alfalfa gathered from the landing site had an unexplained reduction in chlorophyll levels of between 30 and 50 percent. The investigation was unable to find any ordinary explanation for these phenomena. The Trans-en-Provence case has been called the most thoroughly documented UFO sighting of all time. Nicolaï himself, however, did not believe that what he saw was from outer space; he believed that it was a secret French military project.

**SEE ALSO:** The Voronezh Close Encounter (1989)

A WELL-DOCUMENTED OCCURRENCE: This graphic representation depicts the site of a UFO visitation in Trans-en-Provence, France.

# THE PAUL BENNEWITZ
# AFFAIR

Paul Bennewitz was an electronics expert in Albuquerque, New Mexico, who became interested in the UFO phenomenon in the 1970s. In 1979, he began observing and filming strange lights and detecting unusual radio signals above Kirtland Air Force Base. He thought the lights were UFOs and reported them to the authorities at the base. In response, he was invited there to brief several air force personnel on what he had seen.

What Bennewitz did not know is that he was inadvertently snooping on some of the most secret assets of the United States. Kirtland hosts facilities of over 150 federal agencies, including the supersecret National Security Agency. Starting in 1981, according to multiple accounts, the Air Force Office of Special Investigations (OSI) began deliberately feeding Bennewitz false information about UFOs. Two UFO investigators who were also covert OSI assets—J. Allen Hynek and Bill Moore—were recruited to help with this project.

According to the material Bennewitz received, gray-skinned aliens from Zeta Reticuli (referred to as "grays") had an underground base near Dulce, New Mexico, where they brought parts from mutilated cattle and kidnapped humans for bizarre genetic experiments. Conflicts between the aliens and the US government resulted in a violent confrontation at the Dulce base in 1979, which the aliens won. Since then, the US government and other world powers had been trying to find some way to keep Earth from being conquered by the grays.

As this narrative became more paranoid, so did Bennewitz, and he was institutionalized for a period in 1988 and dropped out of UFO research entirely thereafter. Not until after his death in 2003 did the scope of the disinformation campaign against him become clear.

SEE ALSO: Area 51 (1955), The Majestic-12 Papers (1984), John Lear and UFO Conspiracy (1987), The Bob Lazar Disclosures (1989), The Planet Serpo Papers (2005)

MESSAGES FROM THE GRAYS: While at the Kirtland Air Force Base (pictured), electronics expert Paul Bennewitz picked up transmissions that were later revealed to be fabricated by the OSI.

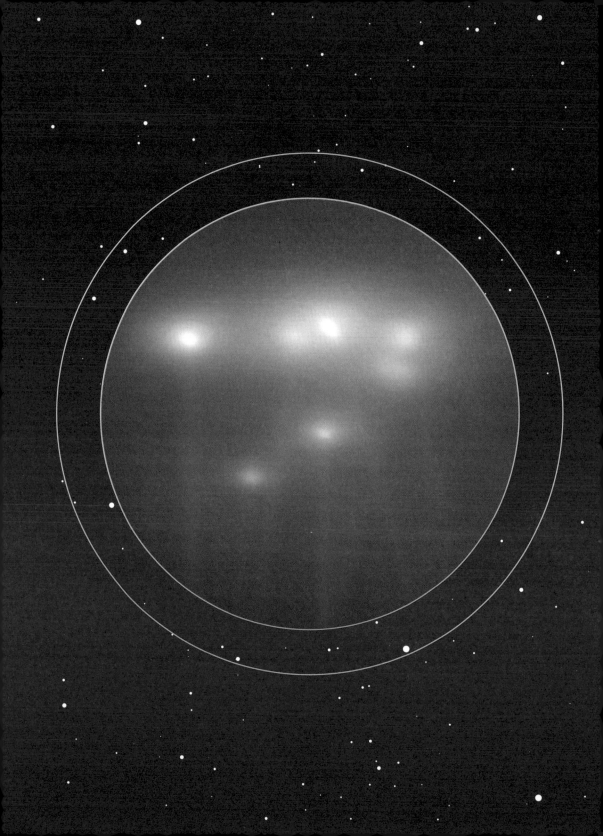

# THE WESTCHESTER
# BOOMERANG

Bill Durkin couldn't believe his eyes. A truck driver by trade, he was headed west on Interstate 84 in the Hudson River Valley in New York on the evening of March 17, 1983. About 8:30 p.m., while he was passing the town of Brewster, he spotted a cluster of lights in the air approaching the highway from the south. The cars around him began driving erratically as drivers pulled over to the shoulder to watch. Durkin did the same.

At first, he thought that he was seeing a commercial jet flying too close to the ground, but he realized it was moving too slowly to be a conventional airplane. He got out and watched as a huge triangular object the size of a football field crossed the highway. It was flat black in color but festooned with multicolored lights. As it flew silently past, Durkin could see what looked like a framework under the craft holding the lights in place. Minutes went by before the object, moving at not much more than a walking pace, vanished from sight to the northeast.

This was the first of dozens of sightings of the object the media labeled the "Westchester Boomerang," after the county in which it was first seen. All through the spring, summer, and early autumn of 1983, it paraded through the skies of the Hudson River Valley and repeated the performances during the same period of 1984. Local authorities insisted that it was merely a group of ultralight airplanes flying in formation—an explanation few witnesses accepted.

The coming of the Boomerang marked an important shift in the phenomenon, however. While most UFOs are seen by individuals or small groups of people, the Boomerang was watched by many thousands. It was the first and one of the most famous of the "black triangles" that became a central part of the UFO experience in the 1980s and 1990s.

**SEE ALSO:** Black Triangles Over Belgium (1989), The Tinley Park Sightings (2004)

BLACK TRIANGLES: What was the Westchester Boomerang? UAP, or ultralight airplane?

SUBJECT: OPERATION MAJESTIC-12 PRELIMINARY BRIEFING FOR
PRESIDENT-ELECT EISENHOWER.

DOCUMENT PREPARED 18 NOVEMBER, 1952.

BRIEFING OFFICER: ADM. ROSCOE H. HILLENKOETTER (MJ-1)

NOTE: This document has been prepared as a preliminary briefing
only.  It should be regarded as introductory to a full operations
briefing intended to follow.

• • • • • •

OPERATION MAJESTIC-12 is a TOP SECRET Research and Development/
Intelligence operation responsible directly and only to the
President of the United States.  Operations of the project are
carried out under control of the Majestic-12 (Majic-12) Group
which was established by special classified executive order of
President Truman on 24 September, 1947, upon recommendation by
Dr. Vannevar Bush and Secretary James Forrestal.  (See Attachment
"A".)  Members of the Majestic-12 Group were designated as follows:

                Adm. Roscoe H. Hillenkoetter
                Dr. Vannevar Bush
                Secy. James V. Forrestal*
                Gen. Nathan F. Twining
                Gen. Hoyt S. Vandenberg
                Dr. Detlev Bronk
                Dr. Jerome Hunsaker
                Mr. Sidney W. Souers
                Mr. Gordon Gray
                Dr. Donald Menzel
                Gen. Robert M. Montague
                Dr. Lloyd V. Berkner

The death of Secretary Forrestal on 22 May, 1949, created
a vacancy which remained unfilled until 01 August, 1950, upon
which date Gen. Walter B. Smith was designated as permanent
replacement.

65-811·10-1

3

# THE MAJESTIC-12 PAPERS

The envelope had no return address and an Albuquerque postmark. It arrived without warning in the mailbox of Jaime Shandera, a Los Angeles–based UFO researcher, on December 11, 1984. Inside was a single roll of undeveloped 35mm film. When the film was developed, it proved to have images of eight typed pages: allegedly a briefing document prepared after the 1952 election for President-elect Dwight Eisenhower, informing him of the secret of the UFOs.

According to the document, the US government had recovered the remains of two crashed flying saucers and the bodies of four humanoid aliens. President Truman then issued an executive order creating a secret committee named Majestic-12, MJ-12 for short, to investigate the alien presence. Shandera and another researcher, William Moore, later found a document in the National Archives that seemed to corroborate the MJ-12 briefing. The documents circulated privately in the UFO research community until 1987, when British researcher Timothy Good was

sent another copy and went public with it, sparking a media firestorm.

Many researchers who examined the documents claimed that they were forgeries, pointing to several significant problems. For example, Truman's signature on the executive order seems to have been pasted in from a photocopy of another, authentic memo; the documents used words and turns of phrase (such as "media" for the press and radio) that nobody used in 1952; and the date format, security classification, and code name assigned to the project violate what was then US government and military practice. Yet the documents reference obscure details about the inner workings of the Truman administration and the US Department of Defense that few people had in 1984. Was it an ordinary hoax, or was it disinformation from within the US government?

**SEE ALSO:** Area 51 (1955), The Paul Bennewitz Affair (1982), John Lear and UFO Conspiracy (1987), The Bob Lazar Disclosures (1989), The Planet Serpo Papers (2005)

QUESTIONS LINGER: These 1952 papers may not have been official government documents, but speculation about their origin remains.

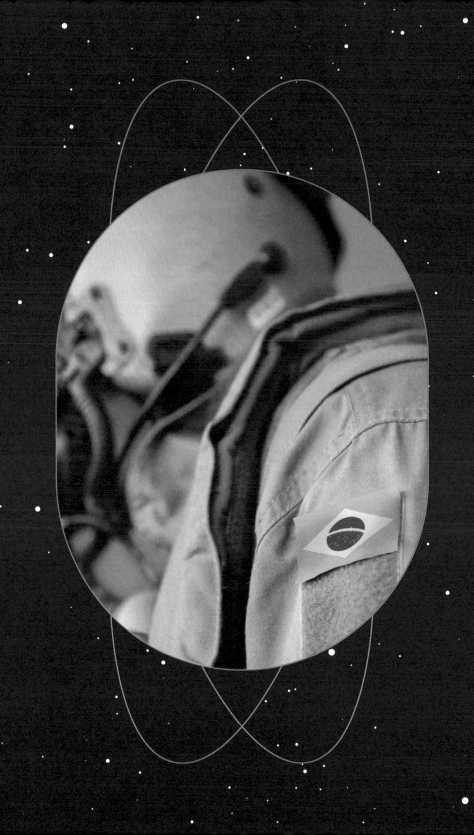

# THE NIGHT OF THE UFOS

The evening of May 19, 1986, began in the usual way at Saõ José dos Campos Airport in Brazil's Saõ Paulo state. At 8:15 p.m., however, air traffic controller Sérgio Mota da Silva noticed three bright red lights hovering above the airport. He picked up binoculars and took a closer look. As he watched, the lights changed color, turning yellow, green, and orange. Guessing the lights might be an optical illusion, he dimmed the runway lights, only to find that the objects came closer to the runway. When he turned the lights back on full, the objects moved away.

He was not the only person to spot something strange in the sky over Saõ José dos Campos. Radar operators at Guarulhos International Airport fifty miles away detected unknown objects in the area at the time of the initial sighting. Meanwhile, Colonel Ozires Silva, the founder of the Brazilian aerospace firm Embraer, was flying back to Saõ José dos Campos from Brasilia. He was at the controls of his plane when he spotted the lights at 9:08 p.m., and tried to approach them. The lights veered away and scattered.

By 9:39 p.m., the Brazilian air force had been alerted, and jet fighters took off from the bases at Santa Cruz and Anápolis not long afterward. Three pilots made visual contact with unknown lights in the sky, but the lights easily outran the fighter planes. One pilot, at the controls of a supersonic Mirage IIIe interceptor, got within two miles of a light, but it zigzagged at high speed and then flew away at a speed the pilot estimated at Mach 15.

The Brazilian air force files on the encounter were declassified in 2009. No explanation for the phenomena sighted that night was ever offered.

SEE ALSO: UFOs Over Washington, DC (1952), The Tehran Sightings (1976), The Manises Incident (1979), The Tic-Tac Incident (2004), The O'Hare Airport Sighting (2006)

RECEBEMOS VÁRIOS RELATOS DE AVISTAMENTOS DE ÓVNIS: In this photo, a pilot's sleeve is pictured with an insignia from Brazil.

# THE FLIGHT 1628 SIGHTING

Japan Air Lines Flight 1628 was a routine cargo flight from Paris to Tokyo following a great circle route that took it over the northern edges of North America. On November 17, 1986, Captain Kenji Terauchi was at the controls of the Boeing 747 cargo plane. At 5:11 p.m. local time, crossing eastern Alaska at thirty-five thousand feet, he sighted three glowing objects keeping pace with his plane. Two of them were small, but the third was gigantic, twice the size of an aircraft carrier. He pointed the objects out to the other two members of the crew, who also saw them.

Six minutes into the sighting, he radioed the Anchorage airport, his next scheduled stop, asking for advice. Officials there advised him to take evasive action. He went to a lower altitude and flew the plane in a circle. The three objects followed the plane through the turns. Meanwhile, the airport radar at Anchorage picked up an object near the 747, and military radars in the same area detected several radar images. The objects continued to follow Terauchi's plane for some four hundred miles before flying off. When Flight 1628 landed at Anchorage, he and the other crew members were interviewed by FAA investigators, who described them as "normal, professional, rational" and found no evidence of drug or alcohol use.

This sighting took place at the height of the 1980s debunking crusade. Unsurprisingly, would-be UFO debunkers therefore vied with each other to explain away the objects the crew sighted, insisting that Terauchi and the other crew members must somehow have mistaken the planets Venus and Jupiter for an object twice the size of an aircraft carrier, and claiming that the radar images detected by civilian and military radars were "clutter." No more plausible explanation for the objects was ever offered.

SEE ALSO: The Chiles-Whitted Sighting (1948), The Nash-Fortenberry Sighting (1952), The Alderney Sighting (2007)

"NORMAL, PROFESSIONAL, RATIONAL": Although the FAA found that Kenji Terauchi and his crew were credible, they brushed away the sighting in this news conference in Anchorage, Alaska, on March 5, 1987.

#1 THE CONTROVERSIAL
NEW YORK TIMES BESTSELLER

# COMMUNION
## A TRUE STORY

# WHITLEY
# STRIEBER

author of TRANSFORMATION

# COMMUNION

The image on the cover burnt itself into the collective imagination of the modern world: an alien being with huge, black, almond-shaped eyes, a pointed chin, and a tiny nose and mouth. Whitley Streiber's book *Communion: A True Story* was the first UFO-related title to feature in the *New York Times* bestseller list, staying there for six months. Its popularity marked a crucial shift in the UFO narrative in the United States and around the world.

Whitley Streiber at that time was best known as a horror writer. According to his account, on several occasions in 1985 he experienced being taken out of his family cabin in the Catskills by alien beings. A series of hypnotherapy sessions in the spring of 1986 under UFO researcher Budd Hopkins's supervision uncovered a cascade of flashbacks of repeated abduction experiences in which he was subjected to medical and sexual experimentation by alien beings. All this, written in vivid novelistic prose, went into the pages of *Communion*.

The results were weirdly reminiscent of the aftermath of Richard Shaver's "dero"

stories. Hundreds of thousands of people wrote to Streiber to recount their own stories of abduction by huge-eyed aliens. Skeptics had a field day, poking holes in various claims *Communion* made and suggesting that Streiber had simply found a more lucrative way to market his horror fiction. Meanwhile, other abductees and UFO researchers, including Budd Hopkins, bristled at Streiber's suggestion that the abduction experience might have a positive dimension.

Streiber wrote five other books on his encounters with aliens, none of them as commercially successful as *Communion*, and went on to become a significant figure in alternative-realities media. In the wake of *Communion*, alien abduction was hardwired into popular culture.

**SEE ALSO:** *The Book of the Damned* (1919), The Shaver Mystery (1945), *When Prophecy Fails* (1954), *Chariots of the Gods?* (1968), *Behold a Pale Horse* (1991)

REVEALED UNDER HYPNOTHERAPY: The eerie face on the cover of Whitley Strieber's *Communion* recreates the memory recovered by the writer after several sessions of hypnotherapy.

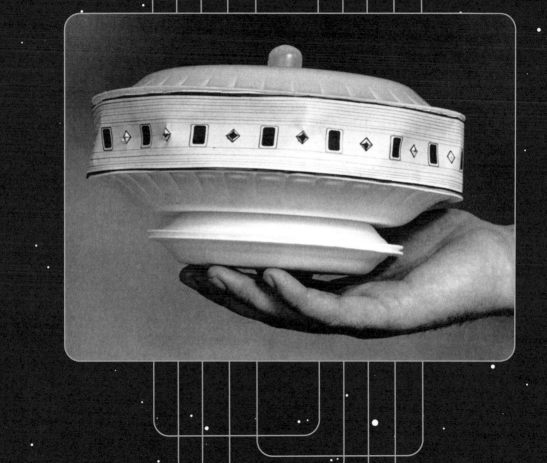

# THE GULF BREEZE ENCOUNTERS

Gulf Breeze is a small suburb of Pensacola in northwestern Florida. On the night of November 11, 1987, according to his testimony, local contractor Ed Walters was working late in his home office when he saw a light shining from above into his yard. He went out to investigate and spotted a glowing top-shaped object in the air. He went back inside to get his Polaroid camera and snapped several pictures of the object, then ran into the street to get closer. Suddenly, a blue-white beam of light shone down on him and lifted him off the ground. A voice said, "Don't worry; we will not harm you." A series of images entered his mind. Then he was blinking awake with no memory of what had happened after the images.

Walters's photos were published a week later in the local newspaper and caused an immediate firestorm of controversy. Several photo analysts claimed that the photos were faked, while thirty other witnesses also reported seeing strange lights. Over the following weeks, Walters reported further encounters with unidentified craft and small, large-eyed alien creatures and published more photographs. Even the UFO research community was divided over Gulf Breeze, with different organizations taking sides for and against the veracity of Walters's testimony.

In 1989, hoping to get away from constant harassment by the media, Walters and his wife moved to another house. In 1990, a new owner bought their old home and discovered a paper model identical to Walters's UFO photos hidden in the attic. Skeptics pointed to this and other evidence to insist that Walters had faked his photos. Walters and his supporters countered by insisting that the model had been planted in the house by skeptics. More than thirty years after the original events, the Gulf Breeze photographs remain among the most controversial of all UFO evidence.

**SEE ALSO:** The Mariana Film (1950), The Ummo Affair (1966), The Tic-Tac Incident (2004)

A GLOWING TOP-SHAPED OBJECT: This model, as seen in a photo taken in the 1980s, approximates the craft seen by Ed Walters.

# THE ILKLEY MOOR CLOSE ENCOUNTER

The moors of Yorkshire in England are desolate stretches of countryside too barren for farming. Ilkley Moor is one of many such places. By the morning of December 1, 1987, it had long been famous among researchers as a place where many sightings of UFOs had taken place. That was when a retired London policeman, Philip Spencer,* set out to walk across Ilkley Moor to visit his father-in-law in a nearby village. Spencer had a camera with him as well as a compass to guide him in the event of fog on the moor.

According to his testimony, partway through his journey, he suddenly spotted a dark greenish figure on the trail ahead. About four feet tall, it had an oversized head and long, spindly limbs. It made a gesture Spencer interpreted as a warning to stay away. Spencer responded by pulling out his camera and taking a photo of the creature. It ran away into the fog, but shortly thereafter Spencer saw a white disklike craft rise up from the moor and soar away into the sky. When Spencer reached a nearby town, the time was two hours later than it should have been, and his compass had been changed so the north end of the needle pointed south.

Once the photo was developed, UFO researchers circulated it to experts, who found no evidence of tampering but noted that it was so blurry that no conclusions could be drawn from it. Spencer later underwent hypnotic regression and described a standard abduction experience in which he was taken aboard a spacecraft and subjected to a medical examination. His encounter is one of the most famous British UFO sightings.

**SEE ALSO:** The Flatwoods Monster (1952), Mothman! (1966), The Varginha Close Encounters (1996)

---

* A pseudonym—the witness insisted throughout the investigations on keeping his real name private.

UPON A BARREN MOOR: The Ilkley Moors in West Yorkshire, England, are a foreboding place.

# JOHN LEAR AND
# UFO CONSPIRACY

The debate over UFOs took a darker turn on December 29, 1987, when John Lear posted a message to ParaNet, an online bulletin board, accusing the United States government of betraying the American people to evil aliens. Lear, the estranged son of multimillionaire Bill Lear, was a professional pilot who had worked for the CIA's private airline, Air America. As an intelligence agency employee and a scion of a very wealthy family, he was seen as an insider by many people, and this gave his accusations more plausibility than they would have had.

Lear's message claimed that governments around the world had been covering up UFOs for forty years, that the Majestic-12 group established by Truman was managing the US response to the aliens, and that the government had obtained several crashed saucers and had carried out negotiations with the aliens. All this, however, was reframed in horrifying terms. According to Lear, the aliens were mutilating cattle, abducting human beings, and carrying out breeding experiments on human subjects in their underground base near Dulce, New Mexico. The government had originally agreed to these actions but was now trying to back out of the deal while still keeping the existence and activities of the aliens secret.

None of this was new. Most of it had already appeared in the aftermath of the Majestic-12 papers or in disinformation given to Paul Bennewitz and passed on by him to the rest of the UFO research community. Nor did Lear have any more evidence for his claims than those previous disclosures had offered. That did not matter. In the cultural context of the late 1980s, as distrust toward the US government became increasingly widespread, it found receptive audiences and helped lay the foundation for even more radical claims to come.

**SEE ALSO:** Area 51 (1955), The Paul Bennewitz Affair (1982), The Majestic-12 Papers (1984), The Bob Lazar Disclosures (1989), The Planet Serpo Papers (2005)

IS THE TRUTH OUT THERE?: John Lear's accusations of alien cattle mutilation were not a new phenomenon, but some believed him due to his family and the cultural climate of the 1980s.

# THE KNOWLES FAMILY ENCOUNTER

The Nullarbor Plain is one of the most desolate areas in Australia, a vast flat desert region with little traffic and few towns. Around 4:00 on the morning of January 20, 1988, Faye Knowles, her sons Patrick, Sean, and Wayne, and their two dogs were crossing that region in her car when they saw a bright light ahead of them, hovering just above the road. As they came closer, they saw that it appeared to be about three feet across, weirdly egg-like, with a yellow center surrounded by brilliant white light. It moved erratically around the road for a time. Then suddenly, it moved on top of the Knowleses' car.

Exactly what happened thereafter is difficult to determine, as the witnesses were terrified and also testified that they became disoriented and their voices slowed down, like a recording played at half speed. They stated later, however, that they heard a clunking sound from the car roof and then felt the car being lifted into the air. Faye and Patrick opened their windows to try to see what the light was doing, letting in clouds of blackish dust and a smell like corpses. Then the car went back down onto the road and one of the rear tires burst. The family fled from the car and hid in low bushes beside the road, but the light was gone.

After fifteen minutes or so, they returned to the car and drove to Mundrabilla, the next town on their route. There and at Cedruna, where the family reported their encounter to the police, witnesses noted that the Knowleses were obviously shaken and found curious black dust all over the car, as well as four odd dents in the roof. A truck driver who had been traveling the same route ahead of the Knowleses' car had also seen a strange light that night, and so did fishermen on a boat offshore to the south. The events of that night remain completely unexplained.

SEE ALSO: The Vilas-Boas Abduction (1957), The Barney and Betty Hill Abduction (1961), The Hickson-Parker Abduction (1973), The Emilcin Abduction (1978), The Zanfretta Encounter (1978), The Cahill Abduction (1993)

BLACK DUST: This is the desolate stretch of Nullarbor Open Road in Western Australia, where an unexplained occurrence came to pass.

# THE VORONEZH CLOSE ENCOUNTER

Many UFO sightings take place in isolated rural regions. The Voronezh encounter is one of the exceptions. Voronezh is a city in southwestern Russia. In 1989, it was a thriving industrial center with nearly a million inhabitants. Beginning on September 23 of that year, many residents observed strange lights hovering over the city. At 6:30 on the evening of September 27, two teenage boys in a city park saw a reddish light in the sky, which descended and became a red sphere thirty feet in diameter. It circled forty feet above the ground and then flew away.

A few minutes later it returned. By then other witnesses had gathered in the park. They watched the sphere descend and a hatch open in the bottom. Two beings emerged. One was humanoid but nearly ten feet tall and wore silver overalls and bronze-colored boots. It appeared to have three eyes and a disk-shaped object on its chest. The other had a rectangular body with arms and legs that moved mechanically; the witnesses thought it was some kind of robot.

A few minutes passed as the witnesses stared. Then the sphere and the two strange visitors suddenly disappeared. Five minutes later the sphere and the tall entity appeared again just as suddenly, but this time the entity had a tube in one hand. It pointed the tube at one of the teenagers, and the boy vanished suddenly. The entity went back into the sphere, which rose from the ground and flew away. At that instant the boy who had vanished suddenly reappeared.

Investigators were able to locate many Voronezh residents who had seen the sphere. They also found four depressions in the ground where the sphere had landed; their measurements showed that something weighing eleven tons had compressed the soil there.

**SEE ALSO:** The Marius Dewilde Encounter (1954), The Straight Line Mystery (1954), The Socorro Landing (1964), The Dechmont Law Close Encounter (1979)

A METALLIC GIANT: Several residents of Voronezh, Russia, witnessed the descent of these ten-foot-tall beings from an unidentified craft.

# THE BOB LAZAR DISCLOSURES

L as Vegas is no stranger to colorful and lurid discoveries, but the one that took place on the local television station KLAS on the night of November 11, 1989, was remarkable even by Vegas standards. That night, a man named Bob Lazar claimed on the air that he had worked on a government program at one of the US government's secret facilities near Area 51, helping to reverse engineer antigravity reactors from crashed flying saucers.

According to Lazar, after graduating from MIT and Cal Tech with degrees in physics and electronics, respectively, and working on several other classified government projects, he had been hired by a secret UFO research program and worked for several years at a facility known as S-4 in the Nevada desert, near Papoose Lake south of Area 51. There he was astonished to see nine UFOs in a secret hangar built into the side of a mountain, and learned that the US government was in possession of alien cadavers.

The crashed saucers, Lazar claimed, came from the Zeta Reticuli system and had been piloted by child-sized, big-eyed gray aliens. They were powered by antimatter reactors fueled by a stable isotope element 115, at that time still unknown to science. They flew by means of gravity wave generators, which could also bend light around the craft for concealment purposes.

Lazar's claims caught the interest of the mass media and ignited a frenzy in the UFO research community, with leading UFO investigators taking up positions both for and against him. His critics pointed out that records of his education and employment could not be verified; Lazar claimed that the records had been erased. As is so often the case, the controversy was never resolved, and to this day UFO researchers in the US remain divided over Lazar's allegations.

**SEE ALSO:** Area 51 (1955), The Paul Bennewitz Affair (1982), The Majestic-12 Papers (1984), John Lear and UFO Conspiracy (1987), The Planet Serpo Papers (2005)

THE SECRET OF S-4: Bob Lazar claimed that the US government was in possession of alien cadavers, but those claims could never be verified.

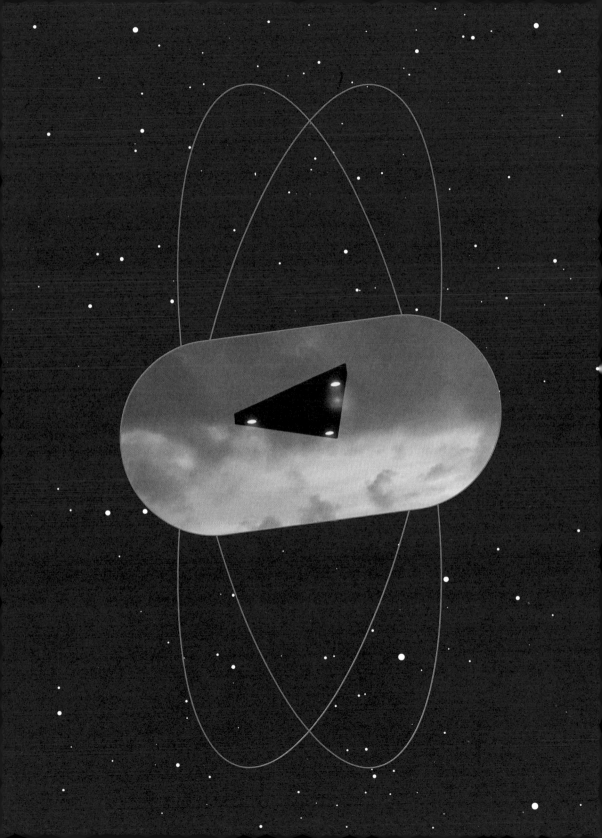

# BLACK TRIANGLES OVER BELGIUM

The most dramatic of the many mass sightings of the black triangle era began on the night of November 29, 1989, over the Belgian town of Eupen, a few miles from Belgium's border with Germany. Two police officers, Heinrich Nicoll and Hubert von Montigny, were on a routine patrol when they spotted an astonishing object hovering over a field: a vast black triangle with brilliant lights at each corner and a red gyrating light like a beacon in the middle. It was motionless when they first saw it, but shortly thereafter flew slowly and silently toward Eupen, where more than thirty other witnesses watched in amazement.

This was only the first of more than two thousand reported sightings of black triangles in Belgium between November 1989 and April 1990. Nearly all the sightings had the same description—a black triangle with brilliant lights at the corners, flying slowly and soundlessly at low altitude. Belgian air force officials suspected that the US Air Force was testing some kind of experimental aircraft over Belgium,

and made inquiries at the US embassy, which were met with the usual bland denials. Meanwhile, skeptics appeared on cue to insist that the triangles were stars, helicopters, or the breakup of a Soviet satellite—none of which convinced those who watched the triangles.

The wave peaked on the night of March 30–31, 1990, when two military radar installations detected an object in the sky over Belgium and several policemen observed the triangle in flight. Two F-16 fighters of the Belgian air force scrambled to try to intercept the object. Despite their best efforts, the pilots were unable to see the UFO, but they had brief radar contacts—and each time this occurred, the object accelerated suddenly at speeds no known aircraft could match. These and the other Belgian triangle sightings remain unexplained.

**SEE ALSO:** The Westchester Boomerang (1983), The Tinley Park Sightings (2004)

THE BLACK TRIANGLE ERA BEGINS: Over two thousand sightings of "black triangle"-shaped craft occurred in Belgium between November 1989 and April 1990.

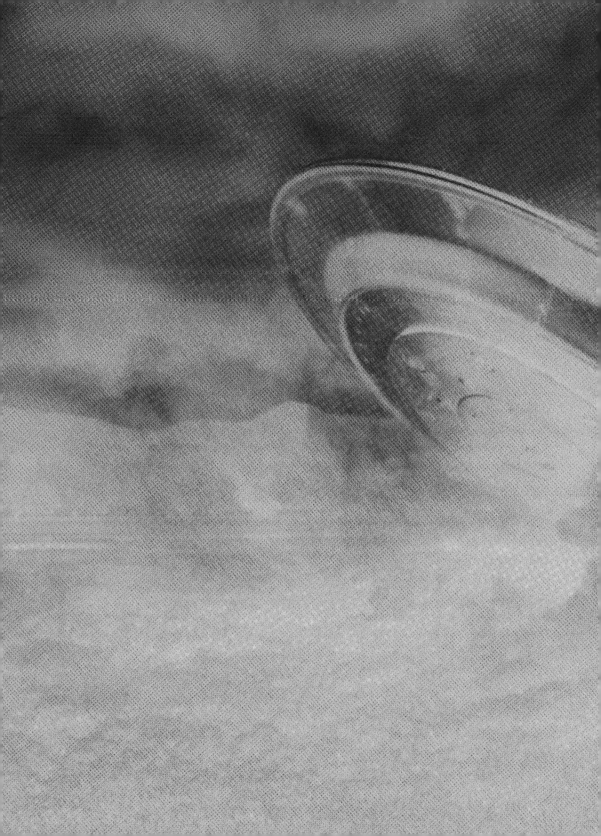

# THE MEGAPLATANOS CRASH

Megaplatanos—for some reason it is usually called "Megas Platanos" in UFO literature—is a village in central Greece about an hour's drive north of Athens. Around 9:30 on the night of September 2, 1990, witnesses in the village noticed six unusual lights moving across the sky from the north. One of them changed colors, wavered in its flight, and then suddenly plunged to the ground, crashing on the slopes of the hill of Tympristos a few miles from Megaplatanos, a short distance from a small church at the crest of the hill.

One witness, shepherd Trantos Karatranjos, was only a quarter mile away from the object when it crashed. He watched it plunge to the ground and burst into flames. As the brush at the crash site caught fire, the other five lights hovered above the crashed object, and two of them suddenly descended. According to Karatranjos, the fires immediately went out. Over the hours that followed, smaller lights, descending and rising again, were witnessed by local villagers.

Once dawn came, a group of local people went to the site of the crash. They discovered an oval burnt area scattered with metal fragments and bits of wire. Police arrived shortly thereafter, and a few hours later a team from the Greek air force drove over from Tanagra Air Force Base to investigate. On October 19, the air force reported that among the debris were fragments of electronic equipment of earthly origin, and the event was officially classified as the crash of a defunct Russian satellite.

This explanation did not satisfy the witnesses, and accusations of a cover-up followed promptly. The Megaplatanos crash has become known as "Greece's Roswell incident." It remains the center of a flurry of claims and counterclaims.

**SEE ALSO:** The Aurora Crash (1897), The Tunguska Event (1908), The Roswell Crash (1947), The Kecksburg Crash (1965), The Shag Harbour Crash (1967), The Varginha Close Encounters (1996)

CRASH LANDING: This unexplained occurrence in Megaplatanos is known as "Greece's Roswell."

# THE CIRCLE MAKERS UNVEILED

The crop circles began to appear in fields in southwestern England in 1978. The first examples were simply circular areas of wheat, barley, or other crops that had been neatly flattened in a spiral pattern during the night. What was causing the circles? Nobody knew, and so speculation ran rampant. Witnesses occasionally saw lights moving in the fields, and that was apparently enough to convince many people that UFOs must somehow be involved.

By 1991, crop circles had become a media circus as well as a reliable income source for farmers in southwestern England, who could make more money from exhibiting crop circles than from selling crops. Tourist buses rolled across the landscape from circle to circle, and souvenir stands sprang up. The crop circles themselves had become more and more complex over time, as though competing for attention. That was when Doug Bower and Dave Chorley went public.

In interviews with the media, they claimed that they had started the phenomenon in 1978 as a prank after reading about the "saucer nests" in Tully, Australia. Using a wooden board, rope, and a simple sighting apparatus, they had learned to gently press down the crops into circles. By 1987, they said, other people had gotten into circle-making. Their announcement was followed by a wave of new crop circles not only in England but also all over the world.

In 1992, alternative researchers Rupert Sheldrake and John Michell set out to settle the matter by holding a contest for the best human-made crop circle with a cash prize. Eleven of the twelve teams succeeded in making crop circles indistinguishable from "real" circles. Believers in a paranormal origin for crop circles argued that this did not prove that all circles had been made by human beings. As with so many other things, the debate remains unresolved.

SEE ALSO: The Mowing Devil (1678), The Tully Crop Circles (1966)

A PRANK ON TRUE BELIEVERS: Whether or not all crop circles were created by humans, there's incontrovertible evidence that some farmers did, in fact, deliberately make them.

BEHOLD A PALE HORSE

WILLIAM COOPER

Lyon
Technology
Publishing

BEHOLD A
PALE HORSE

WILLIAM M. COOPER

# BEHOLD A PALE HORSE

Milton William Cooper was a US Navy veteran who claimed to have witnessed a UFO repeatedly entering and leaving the ocean in 1966, while he was serving in the Vietnam War. In 1988, he began issuing statements on the internet about the same narrative of hostile gray aliens and government betrayal that Paul Bennewitz and John Lear had put into circulation earlier in that same decade. Those became central to Cooper's influential book, *Behold a Pale Horse* (1991). With its publication, the rising tide of UFO conspiracy culture reached full flood.

*Behold a Pale Horse* combined the hostile-alien narrative with nearly every other theme common in twentieth-century conspiracy culture, from the Bavarian Illuminati and the New World Order to the Kennedy assassinations and an imminent ice age. Cooper claimed that President Eisenhower had signed a treaty with the grays permitting them to mutilate cattle and abduct humans in exchange for technology transfers. The aliens, it turned out, were intent on conquering Earth, and so were the Illuminati, setting the stage for a struggle that humanity could only lose.

All of this found plenty of readers across the fringes of the political landscape. *Behold a Pale Horse* became widely read in US prisons, where its popularity provided a crucial text for "lyrical assassins" like the Wu-Tang Clan and Busta Rhymes. Meanwhile, it became just as popular among the nascent militia movement among rural Americans, feeding their conviction that the government really was out to get them.

Cooper himself became convinced that the government would silence him. When he stopped paying his taxes and then opened fire on sheriff's deputies who came to serve a warrant, he made that belief into a reality, and died in a hail of bullets on November 5, 2001. His legacy remains a powerful force in American fringe culture to this day.

**SEE ALSO:** *The Book of the Damned* (1919), *When Prophecy Fails* (1954), Area 51 (1955), *Chariots of the Gods?* (1968), The Paul Bennewitz Affair (1982), The Majestic-12 Papers (1984), John Lear and UFO Conspiracy (1987), *Communion* (1987), The Bob Lazar Disclosures (1989), The Planet Serpo Papers (2005)

VALUABLE INFORMATION: *Behold a Pale Horse* has proven to be an enduring influence on culture, extending as far as the lyrical stylings of ODB.

# THE CAHILL ABDUCTION

Narre Warren North is an ordinary suburb in the foothills of the Dandenong Mountains outside of Melbourne, Australia. On the evening of August 7, 1993, Kelly Cahill and her husband, Andrew, were driving to a friend's house there. A little after 7:00 p.m., she noticed an unusual ring of orange lights in a field. The Cahills left to return home around 11:45 p.m., and when they reached the same place, the ring of lights was hovering above the roadway. The two of them saw that it was a house-sized spherical object with orange lights around the bottom. It vanished at high speed, but a short distance farther on, a bright light suddenly streamed in through the windshield.

Suddenly, the two of them found themselves sitting in the motionless car. They finished the drive home to find that the drive had taken them more than an hour longer than usual. Cahill discovered that she had a strange triangular mark on her belly and suffered unusual menstrual bleeding in the days that followed. For several weeks thereafter, neither of the Cahills could remember what had happened, but—

without benefit of hypnosis—both recalled being approached by strange humanoid creatures with glowing red eyes, and Kelly remembered being taken aboard a UFO. Like other abductees of the 1990s, she also had several later encounters in her sleep, which she described as lifelike dreams.

So far this was an ordinary abduction experience, like those so many others reported during that decade. What makes it one of the most famous Australian UFO cases is that the Cahills were not the only people who encountered a UFO in Narre Warren North that night. Three other people driving through the same area around midnight also saw the same house-sized object with orange lights hovering above the road. Their descriptions corroborate the Cahills' account in every detail.

**SEE ALSO:** The Vilas-Boas Abduction (1957), The Barney and Betty Hill Abduction (1961), The Hickson-Parker Abduction (1973), The Emilcin Abduction (1978), The Zanfretta Encounter (1978), The Knowles Family Encounter (1988)

UNEXPLAINED MEMORIES: Both abductees had hazy memories of the unexplained hour added to their journey.

# THE ARIEL SCHOOL CLOSE ENCOUNTER

Ruwa is a small village in rural Zimbabwe, about fourteen miles southeast of the capital city of Harare. In 1994, it was not much more than a crossroads with a few buildings, but not far away from it is the Ariel School, a private school that draws most of its students from well-to-do families in Harare. At 10:00 on the morning of September 16, 1994, the students were outside enjoying their midmorning recess when a silvery disk appeared in the sky and then settled in an area of brush and small trees just beyond the school grounds. Sixty-two schoolchildren, moved by curiosity, went to investigate.

A group of small, big-eyed creatures dressed in black then emerged from the landed disk. At this point many of the schoolchildren ran away, but some of the older children continued to watch. Some of the children reported sudden intrusive thoughts that seemed to be telepathic communication from the creatures, warning about humanity's abuse of the environment. The creatures then boarded the disk and flew away. When the children went in from recess and told their teachers what they had seen, their account was dismissed as nonsense, but the children told their parents about the sighting that evening. Once word spread, several investigators came to interview the children, and their accounts made the Ariel School sighting one of Africa's most famous UFO encounters.

Like many other close encounters, the events at Ariel School came in the middle of a wave of other sightings: fireballs were seen in the sky in the days beforehand, and several other witnesses elsewhere in the region also encountered strange beings. Some witnesses pointed out, however, that the small, black-clad creatures closely resembled tikoloshes, magical creatures described in the traditions of the Ndebele and Shona peoples.

**SEE ALSO:** Visitors from Magonia (815), Pancakes from Space? (1961), The Westall School Sighting (1966), The Swamp Gas Incident (1966), The Cussac Close Encounter (1967), The Rise of High Strangeness (1969)

HIGH STRANGENESS OR ZETA RETICULI?: A "gray" looks down at the viewer, perhaps as the schoolchildren of the Ariel School saw it.

# THE VARGINHA CLOSE ENCOUNTERS

The city of Varginha in Brazil's Minas Gerais State was once known mostly for its leading role in the coffee industry and its steel and auto parts factories. In 1996, however, a series of highly publicized UFO sightings and close encounters put it on the map as one of Latin America's most famous sites of apparent human-alien contact.

On January 20, 1996, three young women, sisters Liliane and Valquiria da Silva and their friend Katia Xavier, were walking together. Around 3:30 p.m., they saw a strange being huddled against the cinderblock wall of an abandoned building. It had leathery brown skin, a triangular head with large red eyes, and very short limbs. It looked as frightened as they felt, but the young women ran away. When they told their story to the sisters' mother, she and Katia Xavier returned to the place. The creature had vanished, but it left a strong smell of ammonia behind it.

On that same day, according to witnesses, a convoy of military trucks went roaring through Varginha toward an unknown destination. Staff members at a local hospital reported seeing doctors treating figures who did not appear to be human, and military trucks drove up to the same hospital to deliver unfamiliar equipment and a body bag containing a body. Other witnesses reported strange creatures like the ones the da Silva sisters and Xavier had seen.

Claims soon circulated that a UFO had crashed in the area and the Brazilian army had taken four aliens into custody. The Brazilian military denied this and insisted that the witnesses had mistaken a local deaf-mute for an alien. The city government of Varginha responded more practically: a few years after the events, they erected a flying saucer–shaped water tower in the center of the city, and UFO-themed tourism is now an important feature of Varginha's economy.

**SEE ALSO:** The Aurora Crash (1897), The Tunguska Event (1908), The Roswell Crash (1947), The Kecksburg Crash (1965), The Shag Harbour Crash (1967), The Megaplatanos Crash (1990)

3.5 STARS ON TRIPADVISOR: Whether or not an alien truly did crash in this area of Brazil, by all accounts the area around this massive memorial is a pleasant place for a day trip.

# THE HEAVEN'S GATE SUICIDES

The sheriff's deputies were utterly unprepared for what they discovered in the big house in a San Diego suburb: thirty-nine corpses, identically dressed in black tracksuits and Nike running shoes, each laid out neatly on a bed with a purple cloth covering the face. They had killed themselves by taking sleeping pills and vodka and then tying plastic bags over their heads. Thus ended one of the longest and strangest stories in the world of UFO religion.

One of the bodies belonged to Marshall Applewhite, the leader of the group. Born in 1931, Applewhite was a former college professor who had begun teaching his own UFO-based religion in 1972. He and Bonnie Nettles, a nurse turned mystic, came to believe that they were the two witnesses described in the Book of Revelation, and developed a set of teachings that combined Christianity, New Age ideas, and belief in UFOs.

In 1970s counterculture, they had an easy time gathering a circle of followers who believed that Applewhite and Nettles had already achieved an evolutionary level above humanity and hoped to follow them. For the next two and a half decades, the cult—calling itself Human Individual Metamorphosis, Total Overcomers Anonymous, and several other names—led a wandering lifestyle, often living in extreme poverty, while waiting for the aliens to land.

Nettles died of cancer in 1985, and thereafter Applewhite's beliefs shifted in more apocalyptic directions. When Comet Hale-Bopp was discovered, and internet rumors claimed that an alien spacecraft had been sighted following the comet through space, Applewhite became convinced that "Heaven's Gate" was opening for him and his followers. Mass suicide was the way they chose to pass through it.

**SEE ALSO:** The Contactee Era Begins (1952), The Giant Rock Convention (1953), World Contact Day (1953), *When Prophecy Fails* (1954), The Billy Meier Contacts (1975)

A FATEFUL PROPHECY: Cult founder Marshall Applewhite speaks to the camera in his final video message.

# THE TINLEY
# PARK SIGHTINGS

Tinley Park, Illinois, is a suburban town about an hour southwest of Chicago. On the night of August 21, 2004, it was busier than usual: the annual Ozzfest heavy metal festival was just letting out at a big local amphitheater. That was when hundreds of people, local residents as well as concertgoers, noticed three bright lights in a triangular formation in the sky, moving very slowly across the sky without making a sound.

The lights, whatever they were, flew off into the darkness after thirty minutes or so. On October 31, however, they were back, and astonished parents accompanying their children on Halloween trick-or-treat rounds watched, photographed, and filmed the lights. The same thing happened yet again the following year, on October 1 and October 31, 2005. While Tinley Park got the credit, witnesses in the nearby suburbs of Lake in the Hills, Matteson, Mokena, Oak Forest, and Orland Park also reported seeing the lights.

In 1983, when the Westchester Boomerang inaugurated the era of black-triangle UFOs, cell phones with built-in cameras were still a matter for science fiction. In 2004, many of the witnesses had phones in their pockets. Dozens of photos and video clips of the mysterious object promptly found their way onto the internet, making the Tinley Park sightings among the best documented UFO encounters in history.

Careful analysis of the footage from the Tinley Park sightings has shown that the lights appear to have been connected to a very large solid object approximately fifteen hundred feet across. Why the famous black triangle shed all but three of its lights for this appearance remains a mystery.

SEE ALSO: The Stadio Artemio Franchi Sighting (1954), The Boiani Mission Sightings (1959), The Westchester Boomerang (1983), The Voronezh Close Encounter (1989), Black Triangles Over Belgium (1989), The Ariel School Close Encounter (1994)

ALIENS AT OZZFEST: A peculiar light formation was witnessed by a number of concertgoers, and then again on Halloween, amid costumed revelers like this one.

PERSON 1: Look at that thing!

PERSON 2: They're all goin' against the wind. The wind's 120 knots to the west.

PERSON 2: There's a whole fleet of 'em. Look on the SA.

# THE TIC-TAC INCIDENT

The USS *Nimitz* is one of the most powerful naval vessels in the US fleet, a nuclear-powered aircraft carrier bristling with advanced radar systems and weaponry. On November 14, 2004, it was at sea about a hundred miles southwest of San Diego, California, surrounded by the other vessels of Carrier Strike Group 11, on a routine training mission. The weather was clear, with calm seas, and the *Nimitz*'s F/A-18F jet fighters were carrying out aerial drills. Suddenly two of the pilots were instructed to break off the exercise and intercept an unknown object.

For several days, navy radar operators had been detecting unknown objects shadowing the fleet. The objects flew at eighty thousand feet, high above normal jet operating altitude, but now and then one dropped at high speed to lower levels. That was what the two pilots were sent to investigate: an unknown object in the air close to the carrier group.

Commander David Fravor was the lead pilot. According to his report, when he and his wingman reached the scene, they saw a disturbance in the water, with waves churning above something unknown just under the surface. Then a white object shaped like a Tic Tac candy came into sight. About forty feet long, it had no wings or visible means of propulsion but flew at high speed, making sudden evasive maneuvers no conventional aircraft could copy. Fravor tried to intercept it, but it flew straight at him, veered, and then flew away at high speed.

By then other fighters were taking off from the *Nimitz* to intercept the object. One of them, later that day, took a blurry video of the object on an infrared camera mounted on his plane. Leaked to the public in 2017, the video played a major role in bringing about the congressional hearings on UFOs six years later.

**SEE ALSO:** UFOs Over Washington, DC (1952), The Tehran Sightings (1976), The Manises Incident (1979), The Night of the UFOs (1986), Government Hearings on UAPs (2023)

AN UNIDENTIFIED (MINTY?) OBJECT: This video from the USS *Gimbal* is one of three US military videos of UAPs that has been approved for public release by the US government.

# THE PLANET SERPO PAPERS

The documents first appeared on a UFO research forum in November 2005, uploaded by an anonymous poster who claimed to be a whistleblower from the US Defense Intelligence Agency (DIA). They purported to be files from a top-secret US government program that sent twelve astronauts aboard an alien spacecraft to a planet named Serpo, orbiting the star Zeta Reticuli.

According to the Serpo papers, one of the aliens who was aboard the craft that crashed at Roswell in 1947 survived the impact and was taken into custody by the US military. It helped US scientists make contact with its people, called Ebens (Extraterrestrial Biological ENtities) in the papers. After a series of contacts, ten male and two female astronauts boarded an alien spacecraft in 1965 for the ten-month voyage to Serpo.

The papers describe Serpo as a planet with a breathable oxygen atmosphere and slightly lower gravity than Earth. The Eben population of Serpo is around 650,000, mostly living in small villages, though one city exists on the planet. Two of the astronauts died while there and two more remained behind when the remaining eight returned to Earth in 1978; all of the returnees were dead by 2005 as a result of radiation exposure during the interstellar journey.

As with the Project Aquarius and MJ-12 papers, the Serpo documents were closely examined once they were made available to researchers. As with those earlier papers, too, many researchers claimed that the Serpo material was a clever hoax. Investigators pointed out that specific people in the US Air Force Office of Special Investigations (OSI) were involved in all three disclosures. The possibility that these and other seeming leaks may have been part of a broader strategy of disinformation began to be discussed in the UFO research community.

**SEE ALSO:** Area 51 (1955), The Cash-Landrum Encounter (1980), The Paul Bennewitz Affair (1982), The Majestic-12 Papers (1984), John Lear and UFO Conspiracy (1987), The Bob Lazar Disclosures (1989)

A SHOCKING DISCLOSURE: Although some claim that the Serpo papers were a clever hoax, questions remain.

# THE O'HARE AIRPORT SIGHTING

Though UFO sightings became increasingly sparse with the coming of the twenty-first century, a handful of clear and well-documented sightings continued to take place. The O'Hare Airport sighting of 2006 was among the most remarkable of these.

Chicago O'Hare International Airport is one of the busiest airports in the world, and the ground crews there are used to seeing unusual craft overhead. Nobody was prepared, however, for the object that appeared around 4:15 p.m. on November 7, 2006, above Gate C-17. A ground crewman spotted it first while pushing back a United Airlines plane bound for Charlotte, North Carolina, and radioed the crew of the plane. Other United Airlines employees heard the chatter on the radio and ran to look for themselves. More than a dozen people in all saw the object, including pilots, aircraft mechanics, management personnel, and passersby outside the airport.

What the witnesses reported was a disk-shaped craft of dark gray metal hovering in the air above the terminal. The object was completely silent. Estimates of its size ranged from six to twenty feet in diameter. Five minutes after the first sighting, the object shot up through the clouds at high speed, leaving a small, perfectly round hole, which filled in after a short time. However, air traffic controllers in the O'Hare tower claimed that they did not see it, and it did not appear on radar at any point.

The aftermath is in many ways stranger than the sighting. Both United Airlines and the Federal Aviation Administration insisted that no UFO sighting had been reported to them, even though witnesses stated that they had done so. After an investigation by the *Chicago Tribune* forced their hand, it turned out that both were aware of the sighting but insisted that the object was a "weather phenomenon"—a claim that people who had seen the object flatly denied.

**SEE ALSO:** Scandinavia's Phantom Flyers (1933), The Night of the UFOs (1986), The Stephenville Sightings (2008)

INITIALLY DENIED BY THE GOVERNMENT: Because the *Chicago Tribune* published an article in which numerous people spoke about having observed this craft, the FAA did eventually acknowledge it . . . as a "weather phenomenon."

# THE ALDERNEY SIGHTING

At about 2:09 p.m. on the afternoon of April 23, 2007, pilot Ray Bowyer was at the controls of a twin-engine Trislander turboprop plane flying from Southampton, England, to the island of Alderney. Eighteen years of aviation experience made him familiar with most aerial objects but not with the immense shape he saw in the sky over Alderney. He described it as a "cigar-shaped light," gold in color with two black shimmering bands. At first, he wondered if it was an illusion caused by light reflected from greenhouses on the nearby island of Guernsey, but he decided after a short time that it was a stationary object at an altitude of two thousand feet, between ten and forty miles away.

Bowyer grabbed his binoculars and kept the object in sight for nine minutes. He also sighted another similar object farther away. Then the two objects flew off in formation. Two passengers on Bowyer's flight also saw the first object, describing it as "orange" or "sunlight-colored." Another pilot, Patrick Patterson, who was at the controls of another passenger flight at the time, also spotted the object and described it in terms very similar to Bowyer's.

Once he landed in Alderney, Bowyer reported the sighting to the Civil Aviation Authority, characterizing the event as a "near miss." He then flew back to Southampton on the return leg of the flight but did not see the object again. Great Britain's Ministry of Defence, the organization officially tasked with investigating UFOs, displayed its usual sluggishness in this case, stating flatly that it would not investigate the sighting. The British media, on the other hand, gave it plenty of attention, but no one has yet proposed a convincing explanation for the sighting. Bowyer himself never claimed that what he saw was an alien craft. His statement was simply that he had never seen anything like it in fifteen years of flying.

**SEE ALSO:** The Chiles-Whitted Sighting (1948), The Nash-Fortenberry Sighting (1952), The Cressy Cigar (1960), The Flight 1628 Sighting (1986)

A SUNLIGHT-COLORED OBJECT: Alderney Island, pictured here in an aerial photo taken from a plane, was the scene of an unexplained sighting.

# THE STEPHENVILLE SIGHTINGS

Stephenville, Texas, is a two-hour drive north and west of Dallas. It's a farm town that locals, with typical Texas modesty, like to call "the milk capital of the world." On the evening of January 8, 2008, it suddenly became famous for something much stranger. That was when some three hundred local residents saw a huge unknown object in the sky above their town.

Steve Allen, a veteran small-plane pilot, was one of the witnesses. Around 6:00 p.m., he was clearing brush on a hilltop with three other people when a gargantuan object dotted with brilliant blue-white lights came speeding out of the western sky. Allen described it as "bigger than a Walmart," while other witnesses estimated its size as half a mile wide and a mile long. The object slowed over Stephenville and hovered there, while its lights moved in complicated patterns, as though trying to communicate.

Then two F-16 fighter jets came flying over the hill at low altitude, heading straight for the object. As the witnesses watched, the huge object suddenly sped away, moving so fast that it easily outpaced the fighters. Allen estimated the object's speed at more than three thousand miles an hour.

The next day, the local paper published a story on the subject, and dozens more local people came forward saying that they had seen the object and the jets. The air force insisted at first that none of their planes were in the Stephenville area on the night of January 8 and tried to insist the sighting had been an optical illusion. A week later, they changed their story and admitted that there were in fact F-16s over Stephenville that night. Nothing was ever said about what the pilots did or didn't see. Was it a secret government aerospace test, an extraterrestrial craft, or something else? No one outside the US government knows.

**SEE ALSO:** The Stadio Artemio Franchi Sighting (1954), The Boiani Mission Sightings (1959), The Cash-Landrum Encounter (1980), The Voronezh Close Encounter (1989), The Ariel School Close Encounter (1994), The Tinley Park Sightings (2004)

BIGGER THAN A WALMART: This windmill outside of Midland, Texas—"the milk capital of the world"—is just about where small-plane pilot Steve Allen sighted a huge craft.

# GOVERNMENT HEARINGS ON UAPS

What if you announced that UFOs are real after all and nobody believed you? That was the problem that faced the US government in 2023. After more than two decades of increasingly sparse UFO sightings, the government suddenly abandoned its policy of dismissing UFOs as unreal and started admitting that there might be something to all those sightings of the newly renamed UAPs (unidentified anomalous phenomena).

The fun began on January 12 with the publication of the 2022 Report on Unidentified Aerial Phenomena, the product of a new Pentagon office set up the year before to collect sightings. The report included 171 sightings that remained unidentified, and many of those behaved in ways conventional explanations couldn't explain. In July, Congress got into the act with hearings at which two retired military personnel testified to dramatic UAP sightings and a third insisted that the military had recovered crashed UAPs and "non-human biologics."

NASA also joined what was quickly becoming a three-ring circus of bureaucratic not-quite-disclosure. The space agency had set up a study group on UAPs the year before; it held its first public meeting on May 31 and released an initial report on September 14. Like the Pentagon's report, it refused to draw any conclusions but called for more studies.

The media had a field day with all this, but outside of Washington officialdom, remarkably few people were interested. After all those decades in which the US government refused to take UFOs/UAPs seriously and apparently engaged in cover-ups and disinformation, a great many people assumed as a matter of course that this latest change in official policy must also have an ulterior motive. A popular meme summed up the general attitude: "I wanted to believe," it read, "but then the government said they were real."

**SEE ALSO:** Project Blue Book (1952), The Condon Report (1969)

I WANTED TO BELIEVE: Government hearings on UAPs in 2023, pictured here, became a frustrating experience for those who were hoping for a more conclusive disclosure.

# BIBLIOGRAPHY

## 5000 BCE: MYSTERIOUS VISITORS

Coppens, Philip. *The Ancient Alien Question*. Newburyport, MA: New Page, 2021.

Shklovskii, I. S., and Carl Sagan. *Intelligent Life in the Universe*. New York: Holden-Day, 1966.

## 216 BCE: SHIELDS AND LIGHTS IN THE HEAVENS

Mandukian, Marina. "The Wild True Stories of Historical UFO Sightings." *Grunge*. Updated February 13, 2023). Accessed May 2, 2024. https://tinyurl.com/bdh526yf.

Vallée, Jacques, and Chris Aubeck. *Wonders in the Sky: Unexplained Aerial Objects from Antiquity to Modern Times*. New York: Tarcher/Penguin, 2009.

## 815: VOYAGERS FROM MAGONIA

Carter, Jake. "The Strange Link Between Fairies, Aliens and UFOs." *Anomalien*. March 6, 2020. Accessed May 2, 2024. https://tinyurl.com/5h93y4yt.

Vallée, Jacques. *Passport to Magonia*. Chicago: Henry Regnery, 1969.

## 1277: THE BAODING SIGHTING

Chang, Kai-Chi. *From the Record: UFO Sightings in Ancient Chinese History Books*. Taipei: by the author, 1991.

## 1561: BATTLE IN THE SKIES

Black, John. "The Mysterious 1561 Nuremberg Event 'UFO Battle'." *Ancient Origins*. Updated December 7, 2021. Accessed May 2, 2024. https://tinyurl.com/54zxsnb3.

Vallée, Jacques, and Chris Aubeck. *Wonders in the Sky: Unexplained Aerial Objects from Antiquity to Modern Times*. New York: Tarcher/Penguin, 2009.

## 1562: THE DINGHAI SIGHTING

Chang, Kai-Chi. *From the Record: UFO Sightings in Ancient Chinese History Books*. Taipei: by the author, 1991.

## 1639: THE MUDDY RIVER SIGHTING

Anonymous. "First UFO Sighting in America, Muddy River, 1639." *Celebrate Boston*. 2020. Accessed May 2, 2024. https://tinyurl.com/muwyttbm.

## Klein, Christopher.

Klein, Christopher. "America's First UFO Sighting." *History*. Updated January 15, 2020. Accessed May 2, 2024. https://tinyurl.com/2p9kw6e6.

## 1663: THE ROBOZERO SIGHTING

Anonymous. "1663: Robozero, Russia Sighting." *Think AboutIts*. March 1, 2021. Accessed May 2, 2024. https://tinyurl.com/2x4nmxjv.

Vallée, Jacques. *UFO Chronicles of the Soviet Union*. New York: Ballantine, 1992.

## 1678: THE MOWING DEVIL

Anonymous. "1678—Hertfordshire—The Mowing Devil." *Old Crop Circles*. n.d. Accessed May 2, 2024. https://tinyurl.com/bdzp58t7.

Morrison, C. J. "The Mowing-Devil." *Early Modern Pamphlets*. n.d. Accessed May 2, 2024. https://tinyurl.com/3zwne4cx.

## 1803: THE *UTSURO-BUNE* INCIDENT

Lowth, Marcus. "The *Utsuro-Bune* Legend and UFO Encounters of Ancient Japan." *UFO Insight*. Updated October 5, 2021. Accessed May 2, 2024. https://tinyurl.com/yxb6vx4e.

Tanaka, Kazuo. "'Utsurobune': A UFO Legend from Nineteenth-Century Japan." *Nippon*. June 26, 2020. Accessed May 2, 2024. https://tinyurl.com/yf94et2a.

## 1896: THE COMING OF THE AIRSHIPS

Busby, Michael. *Solving the 1897 Airship Mystery*. Gretna, LA: Pelican, 2004.

Krystek, Lee. "The Mystery Airship of 1896." *The Museum of Unnatural Mystery*. 1996. Accessed May 2, 2024. https://tinyurl.com/yc7zfmjw.

## 1897: THE AURORA CRASH

Busby, Michael. *Solving the 1897 Airship Mystery*. Gretna, LA: Pelican, 2004.

McNabb, Max. "The 1897 Aurora, Texas, UFO Crash & the 'Alien' Buried in the Cemetery." *Texas Hill Country*. January 8, 2019. Accessed May 2, 2024. https://tinyurl.com/yupjuz69.

## 1908: THE TUNGUSKA EVENT

Furneaux, Rupert. *The Tungus Event: The Great Siberian Catastrophe of 1908*. New York: Nordon Publications, 1977.

Verma, Surendra. *The Tunguska Fireball: Solving One of the Great Mysteries of the 20th Century*. Cambridge, UK: Icon Books Ltd., 2005.

## 1909: THE RETURN OF THE AIRSHIPS

Gollin, Alfred N. "England Is No Longer an Island: The Phantom Airship Scare of 1909." *Albion* 13, no. 1 (1981): 43–57. https://doi.org/10.2307/4049113.

Watson, Nigel. *UFOs of the First World War*. Stroud, UK: History Press, 2015.

## 1913: AIRSHIPS AGAIN

Holman, Brett. "The Phantom Airship Panic of 1913: Imagining Aerial Warfare in Britain before the Great War." *Journal of British Studies* 55, no. 1 (January 2016): 99–119.

Watson, Nigel. *UFOs of the First World War*. Stroud, UK: History Press, 2015.

## 1914: THE MYSTERY PLANES

Bartholomew, Robert E. "The South African Monoplane Hysteria: An Evaluation of the Usefulness of Smelser's Theory of Hysterical Beliefs." *Sociological Inquiry* 59, no. 3 (July 1989): 287–300.

Watson, Nigel. *UFOs of the First World War*. Stroud, UK: History Press, 2015.

## 1919: *THE BOOK OF THE DAMNED*

Bennett, Colin. *Politics of the Imagination: The Life, Work and Ideas of Charles Fort*. Manchester, UK: Critical Vision, 2002.

Fort, Charles. *The Complete Books of Charles Fort*. New York: Dover, 1974.

## 1933: SCANDINAVIA'S PHANTOM FLYERS

Good, Timothy. *Above Top Secret: The Worldwide UFO Cover-Up*. London: Sidgwick & Jackson, 1987.

Hejll, O. H. "The Ghost Fliers." *Dr. Cagliostro's Cabinet of Curiosities*. May 2, 2011. Accessed May 2, 2024. https://tinyurl.com/mr2cdxpj.

## 1934: CORAL LORENZEN'S FIRST SIGHTING

Hintz, Charlie. "Coral Lorenzen: The Flying Saucer Lady Who Pioneered UFO Research." *Cult of Weird*. n.d. Accessed May 2, 2024. https://tinyurl.com/4axvtuv6.

Lorenzen, Coral E. *Flying Saucers: The Startling Evidence of the Invasion from Outer Space*. New York: Signet, 1966.

## 1938: THE INVENTION OF FLYING SAUCERS

Keel, John. "The Man Who Invented Flying Saucers." In *The Fringes of Reason*, edited by Ted Schultz, 138–145. New York: Harmony Books, 1989.

Nadis, Fred. *The Man from Mars: Ray Palmer's Amazing Pulp Journey*. New York: Tarcher Perigee, 2013.

## 1944: THE FOO FIGHTERS

Anonymous. "The Foo Fighters of World War II." *Saturday Night Uforia*. September 3, 2011. Accessed May 2, 2024. https://tinyurl.com/yjs52w36.

Rendall, Graeme. *UFOs Before Roswell: European Foo Fighters 1940–1945*. Upper Weardale, UK: Reiver Country Books, 2021.

## 1945: THE SHAVER MYSTERY

Shaver, Richard S. *The Shaver Mystery Compendium Complete*. n.p.: Lulu, 2020.

Toronto, Richard. *War Over Lemuria: Richard Shaver, Ray Palmer and the Strangest Chapter of 1940s Science Fiction*. Jefferson, NC: McFarland & Co, 2013.

## 1946: THE PHENOMENON PREDICTED

Layne, Meade. *The Ether Ship Mystery—and Its Solution*. San Diego: Borderland Sciences Research Association, 1950.

Reece, Gregory L. *UFO Religion: Inside Flying Saucer Cults and Culture*. New York: I. B. Tauris, 2007.

## 1946: THE GHOST ROCKETS

Anonymous. "Ghost Rockets." *Historic Wings*. February 26, 2013. Accessed May 2, 2024. https://tinyurl.com/5bubu479.

Anonymous. "The Ghost Rockets of 1946." *Saturday Night Uforia*. September 24, 2011. Accessed May 2, 2024. https://tinyurl.com/5bubu479.

## 1947: THE ARNOLD SIGHTING

Arnold, Kenneth, and Ray Palmer. *The Coming of the Saucers*. Amherst, WI: privately printed, 1952.

Peebles, Curtis. *Watch the Skies! A Chronicle of the Flying Saucer Myth*. New York: Smithsonian Institution, 1994.

## 1947: THE ROSWELL CRASH

Patton, Phil. *Dreamland: Travels Inside the Secret World of Roswell and Area 51*. New York: Villard, 1998.

Saler, Benson, Charles A. Ziegler, and Charles B. Moore. *UFO Crash at Roswell: The Making of a Modern Myth*. Washington, DC: Smithsonian Institution Press, 1997.

## 1948: THE MANTELL INCIDENT

Lowth, Marcus. "The Mantell Incident." *UFO Insight*. Updated October 13, 2021. Accessed May 2, 2024. https://tinyurl.com/2s87vehm.

Stillwell, Blake. "The First Air Force Pilot to Die Chasing a UFO Was Actually Chasing a Secret Balloon." *Military.com*. October 31, 2022. Accessed May 2, 2024. https://tinyurl.com/2byra7tb.

## 1948: THE CHILES-WHITTED SIGHTING

Daugherty, Greg. "Two Pilots Saw a UFO. Why Did the Air Force Destroy the Report?" *History*. Updated January 10, 2020. Accessed May 2, 2024. https://tinyurl.com/36tewf94.

Peebles, Curtis. *Watch the Skies! A Chronicle of the Flying Saucer Myth*. New York: Smithsonian Institution, 1994.

## 1950: THE MARIANA FILM

Keyhoe, Donald E. *Flying Saucers from Outer Space*. New York: Henry Holt, 1953.

Saunders, David R. *UFOs? Yes! Where the Condon Committee Went Wrong*. New York: World Publishing Company, 1969.

## 1952: PROJECT BLUE BOOK

Andrews, Evan. "How the U.S. Air Force Investigated UFOs During the Cold War." *History*. Updated January 15, 2020. Accessed May 2, 2024. https://tinyurl.com/muvfcc3a.

Steiger, Brad. *Project Blue Book*. New York: Ballantine Books, 1976.

## 1952: THE NASH-FORTENBERRY SIGHTING

Nash, William B., and William H. Fortenberry. "We Flew Above Flying Saucers." *True* October 1952. Accessed May 2, 2024. https://tinyurl.com/3cetu2x2.

Tulien, Thomas. "Revisiting One of the Classics: The Nash/Fortenberry UFO Sighting, 14 July 1952." *International UFO Reporter* 27, no. 1 (2002): 22. Accessed May 2, 2024. https://tinyurl.com/5n96hdmt.

## 1952: UFOS OVER WASHINGTON, DC

Randle, Kevin D. *Invasion Washington: UFOs Over the Capitol*. New York: HarperTorch, 2001.

Sullivan, Missy. "In 1952, 'Flying Saucers' Over Washington Sent the Press into a Frenzy." *History*. Updated November 3, 2023. Accessed May 2, 2024. https://tinyurl.com/5n8phue9.

## 1952: THE FLATWOODS MONSTER

Cereno, Benito. "The Bizarre True Story of the Flatwoods Monster." *Grunge*. July 31, 2021. Accessed May 2, 2024. https://tinyurl.com/yuw74hkb.

Guiley, Rosemary Ellen. *Monsters of West Virginia: Mysterious Creatures in the Mountain State*. Mechanicsburg, PA: Stackpole Books, 2012.

## 1952: THE CONTACTEE ERA BEGINS

Adamski, George. *Inside the Space Ships*. New York: Abelard-Schumann, 1955.

Bennett, Colin. *Looking for Orthon*. New York: Paraview Press, 2001.

## 1953: THE GIANT ROCK CONVENTION

Clark, Laura. "Come for the Giant Rock, Stay for the UFO History." *Smithsonian*. January 9, 2015. Accessed May 2, 2024. https://tinyurl.com/yc5rymnf.

Stringfellow, Kim. "Giant Rock, Space People, and the Integratron." *PBS SoCal*. May 15, 2018. Accessed May 2, 2024. https://tinyurl.com/yf4v3h3b.

## 1953: WORLD CONTACT DAY

Bender, Albert K. *Flying Saucers and the Three Men*. London: Neville Spearman, 1963.

Bielawa, Michael J. "Bridgeport's UFO Legacy: Men in Black and the Albert K. Bender Story." *Bridgeport History Center*. n.d. Accessed May 2, 2024. https://tinyurl.com/2bnkxf9n.

## 1954: THE MARIUS DEWILDE ENCOUNTER

Michel, Aimé. *Flying Saucers and the Straight-Line Mystery*. New York: S. G. Phillips, 1958.

Verma, Vicky. "French Railway Worker Claimed Two Martian Visitors Attacked and Paralyzed Him in 1954." *How&Whys*. Updated December 11, 2020. Accessed May 2, 2024. https://tinyurl.com/376kkd3v.

## 1954: THE STRAIGHT LINE MYSTERY

Malin, Josh. "The 1954 French UFO Craze That Led to the World's Weirdest Wine Law." *VinePair*. July 7, 2015. Accessed May 2, 2024. https://tinyurl.com/32bz64mf.

Michel, Aimé. *Flying Saucers and the Straight-Line Mystery*. New York: S. G. Phillips, 1958.

## 1954: THE STADIO ARTEMIO FRANCHI SIGHTING

De Luca, Max. "The Eye in the Tuscan Sky: The Day a UFO Sighting Stopped a Fiorentina Match." *These Football Times*. April 21, 2020. Accessed May 2, 2024. https://tinyurl.com/y5kh4j3b.

Padula, Richard. "The Day UFOs Hovered Over Fiorentina's Stadio Artemio Franchi." *BBC*. January 4, 2013. Accessed May 2, 2024. https://tinyurl.com/2p8x8j7h.

## 1954: *WHEN PROPHECY FAILS*

Festinger, Leon, Henry W. Riecken, and Stanley Schachter. *When Prophecy Fails*. Minneapolis: University of Minnesota Press, 1956.

Moser, Whet. "Apocalypse Oak Park: Dorothy Martin, the Chicagoan Who Predicted the End of the World and Inspired the Theory of Cognitive Dissonance." *Chicago*. May 20, 2011. Accessed May 2, 2024. https://tinyurl.com/w56k4fee.

## 1955: AREA 51

Darlington, David. *Area 51: The Dreamland Chronicles*. New York: Henry Holt, 1997.

Patton, Phil. *Dreamland: Travels Inside the Secret World of Roswell and Area 51*. New York: Villard, 1998.

## 1956: NICAP INVESTIGATES THE PHENOMENON

Hall, Richard H. *The UFO Evidence*. Washington, DC: National Investigations Committee on Aerial Phenomena, 1964.

Jacobs, David M. *The UFO Controversy in America*. Bloomington: Indiana University Press, 1975.

## 1956: THE MEN IN BLACK

Barker, Gray. *They Knew Too Much About Flying Saucers*. New York: University Books, 1956.

Bender, Albert K. *Flying Saucers and the Three Men*. London: Neville Spearman, 1963.

## 1957: THE VILAS-BOAS ABDUCTION

Charbonneau, Jason. "Abduction of Antônio Vilas-Boas, 1957." *Think Anomalous*. September 19, 2022. Accessed May 2, 2024. https://tinyurl.com/234852u5.

Wolchover, Natalie. "The Surprising Origin of Alien Abduction Stories." *LiveScience*. May 11, 2012. Accessed May 2, 2024. https://tinyurl.com/mukwh7dc.

## 1959: THE BOIANI MISSION SIGHTINGS

Greenewald, John. "Father Gill & the 1959 Papua New Guinea UFO Sighting." *The Black Vault*. Updated June 12, 2020. Accessed May 2, 2024. https://tinyurl.com/mukwh7dc.

Lowth, Marcus. "The Boianai Visitants Over Papua New Guinea." *UFO Insight*. Updated September 5, 2020. Accessed May 2, 2024. https://tinyurl.com/3peaufvt.

## 1960: THE CRESSY CIGAR

Anonymous. "1960: The Cressy Cigar." *Think AboutIts*. May 11, 2021. Accessed May 2, 2024. https://tinyurl.com/5n7xfjjf.

Strickler, Lon. "The Cressy 'Cigar.'" *Phantoms and Monsters*. January 16, 2013. Accessed May 2, 2024. https://tinyurl.com/mrpaxxs2.

## 1961: PANCAKES FROM SPACE?

Vallée, Jacques. *Passport to Magonia*. Chicago: Henry Regnery, 1969.

Verma, Vicky. "Bizarre UFO Encounter of US Farmer: Three Aliens Gave Him Pancakes." *How&Whys*. Updated January 29, 2022. Accessed May 2, 2024. https://tinyurl.com/37kvk7zt.

## 1961: THE BARNEY AND BETTY HILL ABDUCTION

Fuller, John. *The Interrupted Journey*. New York: Putnam, 1968.

Wolchover, Natalie. "The Surprising Origin of Alien Abduction Stories." *LiveScience*. May 11, 2012. Accessed May 2, 2024. https://tinyurl.com/mukwh7dc.

## 1964: THE SOCORRO LANDING

Lowth, Marcus. "The Zamora Incident—UFO Landing at Socorro." *UFO Insight*. Updated October 6, 2021. Accessed May 2, 2024. https://tinyurl.com/u3usya9j.

Steiger, Brad. *Project Blue Book*. New York: Ballantine Books, 1976.

## 1965: THE EXETER INCIDENT

Fuller, John. *Incident at Exeter*. New York: Putnam, 1966.

Peebles, Curtis. *Watch the Skies! A Chronicle of the Flying Saucer Myth*. New York: Smithsonian Institution, 1994.

## 1965: THE KECKSBURG CRASH

Dimuro, Claudia. "'Meteorites Do Not Make Abrupt Turns': When a UFO Took Aim at Pennsylvania." *Penn Live*. Updated October 4, 2022. Accessed May 2, 2024. https://tinyurl.com/yzbj92nt.

Kean, Leslie. "Forty Years of Secrecy: NASA, the Military, and the 1965 Kecksburg Crash." *International UFO Reporter* 30, no. 1 (October 2005): 3–9, 28–31.

## 1966: THE TULLY CROP CIRCLES

Anonymous. "1966—Tully." *Old Crop Circles*. n.d. Accessed May 2, 2024. https://tinyurl.com/f4fh9fbm.

Carruthers, Peter. "How Tully Became Queensland's Answer to Roswell." *Cairns Post*. n.d. Accessed May 2, 2024. https://tinyurl.com/4u26hx8k.

## 1966: THE WESTALL SCHOOL SIGHTING

Ryan, Shane J. L. "An Ongoing Mystery: The Westall Flying Saucer Incident." *Kingston Local History*. June 11, 2012. Accessed May 2, 2024. https://tinyurl.com/mry9x7h9.

Sharpe, Matthew. "Westall '66: 50 Years On, Still Stranger Than Fiction." *The Conversation*. April 3, 2016. Accessed May 2, 2024. https://tinyurl.com/2duf4ypd.

## 1966: THE UMMO AFFAIR

Casteel, Sean. "The UMMO Affair: Are Extraterrestrials Living Among Us?" *UFO Digest*. December 31, 2012. Accessed May 2, 2024. https://tinyurl.com/ykz23z7h.

Vallée, Jacques. *Revelations: Alien Contact and Human Deception*. New York: Ballantine, 1991.

## 1966: THE SWAMP GAS INCIDENT

Karel, Joseph Kenneth. "The Famous 1966 Michigan Swamp Gas Case." *Mysterious Michigan*. February 17, 2016. Accessed May 2, 2024. https://tinyurl.com/3dj27s6p.

O'Connell, Mark. *The Close Encounters Man: How One Man Made the World Believe in UFOs*. New York: William Morrow, 2017.

## 1966: MOTHMAN!

Keel, John. *The Mothman Prophecies*. New York: Tor, 1991.

Moore, Nolan. "The Untold Truth of Mothman." *Grunge*. Updated January 23, 2023. Accessed May 2, 2024. https://tinyurl.com/4cvd66w2.

## 1967: THE CUSSAC CLOSE ENCOUNTER

Anonymous. "1967: Cussac, France Close Encounter." *Think AboutIts*. May 2, 2021. Accessed May 2, 2024. https://tinyurl.com/3y6xr5v5.

Lowth, Marcus. "An 'Encounter with Devils' on the Cussac Plateau." *UFO Insight*. Updated September 5, 2020. Accessed May 2, 2024. https://tinyurl.com/yc3hkhbp.

## 1967: THE SHAG HARBOUR CRASH

MacDonald, Michael. "Canada's Best-Documented UFO Sighting Still Intrigues, 50 Years On." *CTV News*. Updated September 21, 2017. Accessed May 2, 2024. https://tinyurl.com/44hp2nnb.

Ricketts, Bruce. "The Shag Harbour UFO." *Mysteries of Canada*. October 30, 2014. Accessed May 2, 2024. https://tinyurl.com/4f5k74ca.

## 1968: *CHARIOTS OF THE GODS?*

Story, Ronald. *The Space-Gods Revealed: A Close Look at the Theories of Erich von Däniken*. New York: Harper & Row, 1976.

Von Däniken, Erich. *Chariots of the Gods?* tr. Michael Heron. London: Corgi, 1971.

## 1969: THE CONDON REPORT

Condon, Edward U. *A Scientific Study of Unidentified Flying Objects*. New York: Bantam, 1969.

Saunders, David R. *UFOs? Yes! Where the Condon Committee Went Wrong*. New York: World Publishing Company, 1969.

## 1969: THE RISE OF HIGH STRANGENESS

Keel, John. *UFOs: Operation Trojan Horse*. New York: Manor Books, 1976.

Vallée, Jacques. *Passport to Magonia*. Chicago: Henry Regnery, 1969.

## 1973: THE HICKSON-PARKER ABDUCTION

Brockell, Gillian. "The Men Claimed They Were Abducted by Aliens. In Mississippi, Police Believed Them." *Washington Post*. June 26, 2019. Accessed May 2, 2024. https://tinyurl.com/4ps6eep4.

Hynek, J. Allen, and Jacques Vallée. *The Edge of Reality*. Chicago: Henry Regnery, 1975.

## 1973: THE CATTLE MUTILATION MYSTERY

Janos, Adam. "The Mysterious History of Cattle Mutilation." *History*. Updated May 31, 2023. Accessed May 2, 2024. https://tinyurl.com/ynkn8bsa.

Kagan, Daniel, and Ian Summers. *Mute Evidence*. New York: Bantam, 1983.

## 1975: THE BILLY MEIER CONTACTS

Kinder, Gary. *Light Years*. New York: Pocket Books, 1987.

Korff, Kal K. *Spaceships of the Pleiades*. Amherst, NY: Prometheus Books, 1995.

## 1976: THE TEHRAN SIGHTINGS

Gomez, Cristina. "Iran's Famous and Documented UFO
   Encounter." *Medium*. January 8, 2024. Accessed
   May 2, 2024. https://tinyurl.com/52xzhc36.

Greenewald, John. "The '1976 Iran Incident.'" *The Black
   Vault*. Updated January 28, 2021. Accessed May 2,
   2021. https://tinyurl.com/2jd667wt.

## 1978: THE EMILCIN ABDUCTION

Kępa, Marek. "A Tale Out of This World: Alien Abduction
   & the Communist Regime." *Culture.Pl*. Updated
   July 16, 2018. Accessed May 2, 2024. https://tinyurl
   .com/5ebpdcsy.

Lowth, Marcus. "Jan Wolski and the Emilcin Alien
   Encounter." *UFO Insight*. Updated September 5, 2020.
   Accessed May 2, 2024. https://tinyurl.com/5n78trd5.

## 1978: THE VALENTICH DISAPPEARANCE

Clark, Jerome. *Strange Skies: Pilot Encounters with
   UFOs*. New York: Citadel Press, 2003.

Serena, Katie. "Inside the Unexplained Disappearance of
   Frederick Valentich." *All That's Interesting*. Updated
   April 16, 2022. Accessed May 2, 2024. https://tinyurl
   .com/5ckzkfce.

## 1978: THE ZANFRETTA ENCOUNTER

Charbonneau, Jason. "Zanfretta Abductions, 1978–1981."
   *Think Anomalous*. May 6, 2017. Accessed May 2,
   2024. https://tinyurl.com/474ych6p.

Di Stefano, Rino. *The Zanfretta Case*. n.p.: CreateSpace,
   2014.

## 1979: THE DECHMONT LAW CLOSE ENCOUNTER

Brocklehurst, Steven. "The UFO Sighting Investigated by
   the Police." *BBC*. November 8, 2019. Accessed May 2,
   2024. https://tinyurl.com/yjyanja6.

MacPherson, Hamish. "Scot's Close Encounter with
   UFO at Dechmont Law Still Baffles." *The National*.
   May 16, 2023. Accessed May 2, 2024. https://tinyurl
   .com/57va3t2s.

## 1979: THE MANISES INCIDENT

Ballester Olmos, Vicente-Juan. "The Manises UFO File."
   *Academia.edu*. n.d. Accessed May 2, 2024. https://
   tinyurl.com/mwr8h2kv.

Vázquez, Galán. "The Manises Case." *Medium*.
   February 7, 2021. Accessed May 2, 2024. https://
   tinyurl.com/bd44xa8s.

## 1980: THE RENDLESHAM FOREST LANDING

Butler, Brenda, Dot Street, and Jenny Randles. *Sky Crash:
   A Cosmic Conspiracy*. London: Neville Spearman,
   1984.

Pope, Nick, John Burroughs, and Jim Penniston. *Encounter
   in Rendlesham Forest*. London: Thomas Dunne, 2014.

## 1980: THE CASH-LANDRUM ENCOUNTER

Schuessler, John. *The Cash Landrum Incident*.
   Stockbridge, MA: UFO Books, 2022.

Wright, William J. "The Terrifying True Story of the
   Cash-Landrum Incident." *Grunge*. December 21, 2020.
   Accessed May 2, 2024. https://tinyurl.com/4ukvdhr5.

## 1981: THE TRANS-EN-PROVENCE LANDING

Lowth, Marcus. "The Trans-en-Provence UFO Landing."
   *UFO Insight*. Updated October 6, 2021. Accessed
   May 2, 2024. https://tinyurl.com/526bfmv8.

Mooner, John. "Documented Alien Craft Landing in
   Trans-En-Provence France." *Medium*. June 21, 2023.
   Accessed May 2, 2024. https://tinyurl.com/25xytywu.

## 1982: THE PAUL BENNEWITZ AFFAIR

Bishop, Greg. *Project Beta*. New York: Paraview, 2005.

Pilkington, Mark. *Mirage Men: An Adventure into
   Paranoia, Espionage, Psychological Warfare, and
   UFOs*. New York: Skyhorse, 2010.

## 1983: THE WESTCHESTER BOOMERANG

Hynek, J. Allen, Philip J. Imbrogno, and Bob Pratt.
   *Night Siege: The Hudson Valley UFO Sightings*.
   St. Paul, MN: Llewellyn Publications, 1998.

Schmalz, Jeffrey. "Strange Sights Brighten the Nights
   Upstate." *New York Times*. August 25, 1984. Accessed
   May 2, 2024. https://tinyurl.com/3dfzhyar.

## 1984: THE MAJESTIC-12 PAPERS

Pilkington, Mark. *Mirage Men: An Adventure into
   Paranoia, Espionage, Psychological Warfare, and
   UFOs*. New York: Skyhorse, 2010.

Wood, Dr. Robert, and Ryan S. Wood. "The Majestic
   Documents." *Majestic Documents*. n.d. Accessed
   May 2, 2024. https://tinyurl.com/2kx566jd.

## 1986: THE NIGHT OF THE UFOS

Government of Brazil. "Official UFO Night in Brazil." *Gov.br*. Updated May 20, 2022. Accessed May 2, 2024. https://tinyurl.com/3bnssyac.

Reid, Claire. "Brazilian Air Force Pilots Chase '15,000mph Craft' in 'Night of the UFOs.'" *Unilad*. June 24, 2022. Accessed May 2, 2024. https://tinyurl.com/2vjzv3c7.

## 1986: THE FLIGHT 1628 SIGHTING

Carter, Jake. "Flight 1628 UFO Incident Over Alaska." *Anomalien*. October 3, 2019. Accessed May 2, 2024. https://tinyurl.com/4jaw4kpc.

Weiss, Lawrence D. "Unfriendly Skies: The Extraordinary Flight of JAL 1628, Alaska's Best Known UFO Encounter." *Anchorage Press*. Updated September 17, 2022. Accessed May 2, 2024. https://tinyurl.com/24etab3c.

## 1987: *COMMUNION*

Conroy, Ed. *Report on Communion*. New York: William Morrow, 1989.

Streiber, Whitley. *Communion*. New York: Avon: 1987.

## 1987: THE GULF BREEZE ENCOUNTERS

Myers, Craig R. *War of the Words: The True but Strange Story of the Gulf Breeze UFO*. n.p.: Xlibris, 2006.

Walters, Ed, and Frances Walters. *The Gulf Breeze Sightings*. New York: William Morrow, 1990.

## 1987: THE ILKLEY MOOR CLOSE ENCOUNTER

Carter, Jake. "The Ilkley Moor Alien." *Anomalien*. January 5, 2015. Accessed May 2, 2024. https://tinyurl.com/bdd2wz8e.

Redfern, Nick. *Top Secret Alien Abduction Files: What the Government Doesn't Want You to Know*. Newburyport, MA: Red Wheel Weiser, 2018.

## 1987: JOHN LEAR AND UFO CONSPIRACY

Peebles, Curtis. *Watch the Skies! A Chronicle of the Flying Saucer Myth*. New York: Smithsonian Institution, 1994.

Pilkington, Mark. *Mirage Men: An Adventure into Paranoia, Espionage, Psychological Warfare, and UFOs*. New York: Skyhorse, 2010.

## 1988: THE KNOWLES FAMILY ENCOUNTER

Knibb, Ashley. "Looking at the Knowles Family UFO Encounter." *Ashley Knibb*. January 19, 2020. Accessed May 2, 2024. https://tinyurl.com/47txstzt.

North, Jen. "The Nullarbor Plain UFO Incident." *Medium*. April 20, 2023. Accessed May 2, 2024. https://tinyurl.com/3vev9c7x.

## 1989: THE VORONEZH CLOSE ENCOUNTER

Fein, Esther B. "U.F.O. Landing Is Fact, Not Fantasy, the Russians Insist." *New York Times*. October 11, 1989. Accessed May 2, 2024. https://tinyurl.com/mtn22e3a.

Vallée, Jacques. *UFO Chronicles of the Soviet Union*. New York: Ballantine, 1992.

## 1989: THE BOB LAZAR DISCLOSURES

Patton, Phil. *Dreamland: Travels Inside the Secret World of Roswell and Area 51*. New York: Villard, 1998.

Pilkington, Mark. *Mirage Men: An Adventure into Paranoia, Espionage, Psychological Warfare, and UFOs*. New York: Skyhorse, 2010.

## 1989: BLACK TRIANGLES OVER BELGIUM

Daugherty, Greg, and Missy Sullivan. "Huge, Hovering and Silent: The Mystery of 'Black Triangle' UFOs." *History*. July 22, 2020. Accessed May 2, 2024. https://tinyurl.com/4hhnc2fd.

## 1990: THE MEGAPLATANOS CRASH

Lowth, Marcus. "The UFO Crash at Megas Platanos, Greece." *UFO Insight*. Updated October 13, 2021. Accessed May 2, 2024. https://tinyurl.com/5hx7293b.

## 1991: THE CIRCLE MAKERS UNVEILED

Schnabel, Jim. *Round in Circles*. London: Penguin, 1994.

Silva, Freddy. *Secrets of the Fields*. Newburyport, MA: Hampton Roads, 2002.

## 1991: *BEHOLD A PALE HORSE*

Cooper, Milton William. *Behold a Pale Horse*. Flagstaff, AZ: Light Technology Publishing, 1991.

Jacobson, Mark. *Pale Horse Rider: William Cooper, the Rise of Conspiracy, and the Fall of Trust in America*. New York: Blue Rider Press, 2018.

## 1993: THE CAHILL ABDUCTION

Greenewald, John. "Kelly Cahill Abduction, Dandenong Foothills, Australia—August 8, 1993." *The Black Vault*. June 21, 2021. Accessed May 2, 2024. https://tinyurl.com/2ztrme2r.

Neal, Matt. "'Holy Grail' or Epic Hoax? Australian Kelly Cahill's UFO Abduction Story Still Stirs Passions." *ABC News*. Updated September 26, 2020. Accessed May 2, 2024. https://tinyurl.com/2t7h64z4.

## 1994: THE ARIEL SCHOOL CLOSE ENCOUNTER

Lowth, Marcus. "The Still Unexplained 1994 Ariel School UFO Alien Encounter." *UFO Insight*. Updated September 5, 2020. Accessed May 2, 2024. https://tinyurl.com/2wmtx5sm.

Mahoney, Ellen. "Through Their Eyes—the Ariel School Encounter." *JAR*. June 28, 2018. Accessed May 2, 2024. https://tinyurl.com/mr2xbyew.

## 1996: THE VARGINHA CLOSE ENCOUNTERS

Carter, Jake. "Varginha UFO Incident: Brazilian Military Captured 'Alien Humanoids' in 1996." *Anomalien*. March 7, 2020. Accessed May 2, 2024. https://tinyurl.com/4bmnhf49.

Guevara, Oshea. "The Varginha UFO Incident: Unraveling the Enigma of Extraterrestrial Encounter." *Medium*. July 13, 2023. Accessed May 2, 2024. https://tinyurl.com/398hbxk2.

## 1997: THE HEAVEN'S GATE SUICIDES

Anglis, Jacklyn. "The Twisted Story of the Heaven's Gate Cult—and Their Tragic Mass Suicide." *All That's Interesting*. Updated November 7, 2023. Accessed May 2, 2024. https://tinyurl.com/399y5nke.

Zeller, Benjamin E. *Heaven's Gate: America's UFO Religion*. New York: New York University Press, 2014.

## 2004: THE TINLEY PARK SIGHTINGS

Holliday, Doc. "When Hundreds in Illinois Saw the Same Massive UFO Twice." *100.9 The Eagle*. August 8, 2023. Accessed May 2, 2024. https://tinyurl.com/4kmn5ujw.

Lowth, Marcus. "UFOs Over Illinois—The O'Hare, Tinley Park, and St. Clair Sightings." *UFO Insight*. Updated November 9, 2021. Accessed May 2, 2024. https://tinyurl.com/y8f6w5br.

## 2004: THE TIC-TAC INCIDENT

Chasan, Aliza. "The Story Behind the 'Tic Tac' UFO Sighting by Navy Pilots in 2004." *CBS News*. July 26, 2023. Accessed May 2, 2024. https://tinyurl.com/4bawvhue.

Daugherty, Greg. "When Top Gun Pilots Tangled with a Baffling Tic-Tac-Shaped UFO." *History*. Updated October 2, 2023. Accessed May 2, 2024. https://tinyurl.com/4hvy688e.

## 2005: THE PLANET SERPO PAPERS

Didymus, John Thomas. "NASA Allegedly Sent Human Astronauts to an Alien Planet in 1965." *Inquisitr*. August 13, 2015. Accessed May 2, 2024. https://tinyurl.com/yvsrftz6.

Kasten, Len. *Secret Journey to Planet Serpo: A True Story of Interplanetary Travel*. Rochester, VT: Inner Traditions, 2013.

## 2006: THE O'HARE AIRPORT SIGHTING

Anonymous. "Chicago O'Hare UFO Incident." *The UFO Database*. n.d. Accessed May 2, 2024. https://tinyurl.com/469mhavh.

## 2007: THE ALDERNEY SIGHTING

Anonymous. "Pilot Spots 'UFO' Over Guernsey." *BBC*. Updated April 25, 2007. Accessed May 2, 2024. https://tinyurl.com/59smcwrn.

Haines, Lester. "UK Airline Pilots Spot Giant UFO." *The Register*. April 27, 2007. Accessed May 2, 2024. https://tinyurl.com/29znba56.

## 2008: THE STEPHENVILLE SIGHTINGS

Janowitz, Nathaniel. "15 Years Ago, UFO Sightings Rocked a Small Texas Town. The Mystery Remains." *Vice*. September 29, 2023. Accessed May 2, 2024. https://tinyurl.com/h3fcdzet.

Kennedy, William. "Inside the Stephenville, Texas UFO Sightings of 2008." *Grunge*. September 20, 2023. Accessed May 2, 2024. https://tinyurl.com/52njemum.

## 2023: GOVERNMENT HEARINGS ON UAPS

Cooper, Helene. "Lawmakers and Former Officials Press for Answers on U.F.O.s." *New York Times*. July 26, 2023. Accessed May 2, 2024. https://tinyurl.com/34rwsz3p.

# IMAGE CREDITS

# INDEX

# ABOUT THE AUTHOR

Sara Greer

Born in the gritty navy town of Bremerton, Washington, and raised in the south Seattle suburbs, **JOHN MICHAEL GREER** began writing about as soon as he could hold a pencil. He lives in Cumberland, Maryland, with his spouse, Sara; serves as presiding officer of the Ancient Order of Druids in America (AODA), a Druid order founded in 1912; and writes in half a dozen nonfiction fields, nearly all of them focused on the revival of forgotten ideas, insights, and traditions of practice from the rubbish heap of history. He also runs the unexplained-phenomena blog Ecosophia, which receives over 150,000 visitors per month.

Find him online at Ecosophia.net.